CAMPAIGN 276

WATERLOO 1815 (1)

Quatre Bras

JOHN FRANKLIN

ILLUSTRATED BY GERRY EMBLETON

Series editor Marcus Cowper

First published in Great Britain in 2014 by Osprey Publishing,
PO Box 883, Oxford, OX1 9PL, UK
1385 Broadway, 5th Floor, New York, NY 10018, USA
E-mail: info@ospreypublishing.com

© 2014 Osprey Publishing Ltd
Osprey Publishing is part of Bloomsbury Publishing Plc

A CIP catalogue record for this book is available from the British Library.

ISBN: 978 1 4728 0363 4
E-book ISBN: 978 1 4728 0364 1
E-pub ISBN: 978 1 4728 0365 8

Editorial by Ilios Publishing Ltd, Oxford, UK (www.iliospublishing.com)
Index by Mark Swift
Typeset in Myriad Pro and Sabon
Maps by Bounford.com
3D bird's-eye view by The Black Spot
Battlescene illustrations by Gerry Embleton
Originated by PDQ Media, Bungay, UK
Printed in China through Worldprint Ltd.

16 17 18 10 9 8 7 6 5 4

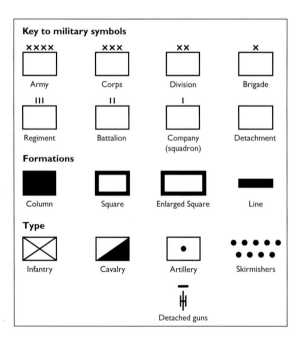

Key to military symbols

xxxx	xxx	xx	x
Army	Corps	Division	Brigade
III	II	I	
Regiment	Battalion	Company (squadron)	Detachment

Formations

Column	Square	Enlarged Square	Line

Type

Infantry	Cavalry	Artillery	Skirmishers
		Detached guns	

AUTHOR'S NOTE

French was the international language in 1815. To ensure that the narrative
within this publication retains a contemporary quality, a number of
conventions have been adopted. This is especially relevant to the French
and Prussian ranks and regimental designations. Wherever possible the
original terminology has been employed, while that used for the Allied
Army is exclusively British.

French terminology includes:

Maréchal	Field Marshal
Lieutenant-général	Lieutenant-General
Maréchal-de-camp	Major-General
Chef-de-bataillon	Infantry Major
Chef d'escadron	Cavalry Major
Garde Impériale	Imperial Guard
Vieille Garde	Old Guard
Jeune Garde	Young Guard
d'Infanterie de Ligne	Line Infantry
d'Infanterie Léger	Light Infantry
Artillerie à Pied	Foot Artillery
Artillerie à Cheval	Horse Artillery
Lanciers	Lancers
Sapeurs	Engineers
Tirailleurs	Skirmishers

Prussian terminology includes:

Feldmarschall	Field Marshal
Generallieutnant	Lieutenant-General
Generalmajor	Major-General
Oberst	Colonel
Oberstlieutnant	Lieutenant-Colonel
Rittmeister	Cavalry Captain
Kurmärkisches	Kurmark
Neumärkisches	Neumark
Schlesisches	Silesian
Westphälisches	Westphalian
Westpreußisches	West Prussian
Fußbatterie	Foot Artillery
Reitende Batterie	Horse Artillery
Schützen	Riflemen
Uhlan	Lancer

ACKNOWLEDGEMENT

It would not have been possible to produce this volume without the
assistance of a considerable number of individuals who, over many years,
have made important new material on the campaign available to my study.
I would particularly like to thank Paul Dawson and Mike Robinson, André
Dellevoet and Erwin Muilwijk for their invaluable contributions to my
understanding of the events at Quatre Bras.

ARTIST'S NOTE

Readers may care to note that the original paintings from which the colour
plates in this book were prepared are available for private sale. The
Publishers retain all reproduction copyright whatsoever. All enquiries
should be addressed to:

www.gerryembleton.com

The Publishers regret that they can enter into no correspondence upon this
matter.

THE WOODLAND TRUST

Osprey Publishing are supporting the Woodland Trust, the UK's leading
woodland conservation charity, by funding the dedication of trees.

CONTENTS

INTRODUCTION

At the pinnacle of his power Emperor Napoleon Bonaparte was master of Europe, but by the spring of 1814 he had been forced to abdicate the throne of France by the coalition united against him, and a revolt by several of his marshals. Accompanied by a small garrison, he was exiled to the tiny island of Elba to brood upon his misfortune and the perceived betrayal which led to his downfall.

With the emperor banished, the major powers opposed to France arranged the return of the former Bourbon King, Louis XVIII, an act ratified at the end of May by the signing of the Treaty of Paris. The sovereigns of Austria, Britain, Prussia and Russia, and their allies in Portugal, Spain and Sweden, heralded this deed as marking an end to tyranny. However, the euphoria of victory evaporated with the realization of the cost of the long struggle with France. The belligerents and the ambassadors from several of the smaller German states subsequently gathered in Vienna to discuss the terms of the settlement to be imposed upon the French nation, including the ceding of colonies and territory. It was agreed that France would retain the land and borders it possessed on 1 January 1792, and that the map of Europe would be redrawn accordingly. The great powers now vied for territorial gains, and the ensuing political machinations resulted in deep divisions and mistrust. This was particularly evident with the circumstances pertaining to the newly created Kingdom of the United Netherlands under the rule of the House of Orange-Nassau.

The Congress of Vienna was convened in September 1814 by the sovereigns and statesmen of the leading European powers in order to settle the issues arising from the long war with France. Painting by Jean-Baptiste Isabey. (The Granger Collection, New York)

THE LIBERATION OF BELGIUM AND HOLLAND

Following Napoleon's defeat at the battle of Leipzig in October 1813 the exiled Dutch Prince Willem VI seized the opportunity to regain power in his homeland and to make further territorial claims. The former Austrian dominion of Belgium had been an integral part of France since 1795, while Holland had been annexed in 1810, but as the French fled from Germany and the northern provinces for the haven of their fortresses in the south, Willem returned to The Hague and boldly established his royal court, proclaiming himself Sovereign Prince. This met with the approval of the British Minister for Foreign Affairs, Viscount Castlereagh, who was fearful of Prussian territorial expansion towards the Meuse River and the influence that they would then command in the region. The British government granted Willem the title and augmented his realm with the town of Antwerp in an attempt to safeguard the vital port. An expeditionary force of British and Hanoverian troops under Sir Thomas Graham, later Lord Lynedoch, was hastily dispatched to support the new regime in its efforts to liberate the country from the remaining French garrisons, as well as to protect it from the marauding Prussians under Generallieutenant Freiherr von Bülow, Graf von Dennewitz, who had advanced into the heart of the Ardennes in the wake of the Cossacks, Austrians and Swedes.

The Sovereign Prince declared himself King Willem I of the United Netherlands and Grand Duke of Luxembourg. Painting by Joseph Paelinck. (Rijksmuseum, Amsterdam)

Adhering to the formal protocols, Castlereagh sought diplomatic support for the Dutch crown from the leading Austrian statesman, Klemens, Fürst von Metternich, as Austria had a historical claim to the land. Metternich duly consented, subject to reciprocal British patronage for Austrian territorial claims in Poland and northern Italy. By the end of January 1814 support had been gained from the remaining coalition members, with the notable exception of the Prussian plenipotentiary, Karl August, Fürst von Hardenberg. However, Willem was not satisfied. He sought to enlarge the kingdom with additional territory and to re-establish his nation as a colonial power. He demanded Luxemburg and the fertile land between the Meuse, Moselle and the Rhine. This conflicted with the Prussians' desire to regain their former lands, and so as compensation Willem was given the Belgian provinces to the west of the Meuse. Britain agreed to return almost all of the Dutch colonies it had taken during the wars with France in return for the new government strengthening the line of fortresses along its southern border, and thereby providing greater protection against possible French aggression. Each of these issues was debated at the Congress of Vienna, where the Duke of Wellington replaced Viscount Castlereagh as Britain's representative. But unbeknown to the delegates another event would dramatically alter the situation in Europe. For on 26 February 1815, Napoleon escaped from Elba.

THE COALITION PREPARES TO INVADE FRANCE

News of Napoleon's escape reached Vienna during the evening of 7 March, and was immediately communicated to the sovereigns and statesmen who were engaged in the negotiations at the congress. They all agreed to wait for further intelligence before formulating a response. But subsequent reports from Genoa confirmed that Napoleon had landed at Golfe Juan on 1 March and, having failed to gain possession of the fortress at Antibes, had continued towards Grasse. The plenipotentiaries of the eight powers who had signed the Treaty of Paris assembled that evening and resolved to publish a declaration in which they affirmed to maintain the peace. The declaration was duly published, and on 25 March, five days after Napoleon had entered Paris to popular acclaim, it was formally ratified as the Treaty of Chaumont. Under the terms agreed the Allied powers would mobilize 700,000 men, commanded by Feldmarschall Karl Philipp, Fürst zu Schwarzenberg of Austria, and a massive concentration of manpower would take place along the French frontier. However, it would take several months before the entire force could be assembled.

Lord Robert Stewart, 2nd Viscount Castlereagh, was the British Minister for Foreign Affairs and Plenipotentiary to the Congress of Vienna between September 1814 and February 1815. Painting by Sir Thomas Lawrence. (The Granger Collection, New York)

The Prussians were to raise an army of 150,000 men on the lower Rhine. These would be led by Feldmarschall Gebhard Lebrecht, Fürst Blücher von Wahlstadt, while the Duke of Wellington was appointed to the command of the British, Dutch and Belgian forces stationed in the Low Countries. Britain did not have a large army, and many of its experienced soldiers were in America. Subsequently, it was stipulated that in lieu of a substantial military force Britain was to provide subsidies, and to raise additional troops from the smaller German states. The latter arrangement proved complex and lengthy discussions ensued as the Prussians called for many of these troops to be placed under their command. It was eventually agreed that the Brunswick, Hanoverian and Nassau contingents would join the troops under the Duke of Wellington, and on 29 March the duke left Vienna for Brussels.

The news of Napoleon's escape from Elba had arrived in the Belgian capital on 11 March, and many of those in the city, including the British civilian population, became apprehensive at the prospect of military operations. However, attention was diverted on the 17th when the mayor read a proclamation from the balcony of the Hôtel de Ville, informing the people that the Congress of Vienna had agreed upon the union of the former United Provinces and Austrian Netherlands, and subsequently the Sovereign Prince declared himself King Willem I of the United Netherlands and pronounced his eldest son the Hereditary Prince of Orange-Nassau.

During the course of the night of 4 April, the Duke of Wellington arrived in Brussels and established his headquarters on the rue Royale. Almost immediately he attempted to seize the reins of military power, but was thwarted by the king, who stated that his army had been placed under the command of the Prince of Orange-Nassau and was to remain a separate entity. In addition, the duke was astonished by the parlous state of the British contingent, and it was evident that a Herculean effort would be required to turn the peacetime garrison into an effective army. Undaunted by the political delicacies, the duke issued a General Order, whereby he assumed the command of the British and Hanoverian troops in the Low Countries, and began to reorganize the Allied Army and to secure trusted subordinates for the various staff positions. New plans were formulated for the defence of the realm. He toured the frontier, accompanied by King Willem, and a memorandum was prepared on the condition of the fortresses and the appropriate strength and composition of the garrisons. Dutch and Belgian troops were stationed in Ath, Ghent, Mons and Tournai, while the four brigades of the Hanoverian Reserve Corps, under Lieutenant-General Count Friedrich von der Decken, occupied Antwerp, Ostend, Nieuport and Ypres respectively. A hectic round of reviews and inspections followed, and at the end of the month the duke informed his senior subordinates of the plan of campaign in the event of an enemy attack.

The delegates at the Congress of Vienna agreed upon the union of the former United Provinces and Austrian Netherlands as a single realm under the rule of the House of Orange-Nassau. Painting from the Ullstein Bild. (The Granger Collection, New York)

While the Allied Army made its preparations for war, the Prussians under Feldmarschall Blücher, in partnership with Generallieutenant August, Graf Neidhardt von Gneisenau, had steadily increased in size. A large proportion of the Prussian Army was made up of conscripts with no experience, although the majority of the officers were veterans. Yet there were problems with the Saxon troops, who objected to being made to serve under the Prussians, and when orders were issued to divide the Saxon force, they mutinied. Drastic measures were adopted by the Prussian high command to redeem the situation, and eventually most of the Saxon contingent was removed. The political intrigues which had preceded this rebellion led several members of the Prussian hierarchy, particularly Gneisenau, to view their allies with extreme caution. However, Blücher's fervour was undiminished, and on 3 May a conference was held at Tirlemont between the Prussian marshal and the Duke of Wellington to agree upon a strategy of cooperation. The two commanders made arrangements for the rapid concentration of their armies, and subsequently the Prussians moved forward, so as to guard the eastern half of the Low Countries.

To ensure that the two armies continued to act in concert, military commissioners were sent to the opposite headquarters: Lieutenant-Colonel Sir Henry Hardinge, 1st Foot Guards, went to Namur, and Generalmajor Karl, Freiherr von Müffling joined the duke and his staff in Brussels. The Prussians made it known that they were anxious to take the offensive, because of the supply problems they were encountering. But the duke persuaded them to remain in their cantonments and to await the arrival of the Austrians and the Russians, for when the coalition armies were assembled, they would take the field in such overwhelming numbers as to gain a decisive victory.

By the beginning of May the threat of imminent military operations had subsided, and an air of uncertainty prevailed. On the 7th, King Willem issued a decree appointing the Duke of Wellington Field Marshal of the Netherlands Army, thereby fulfilling the formal prerogatives, while placing the senior and most experienced Allied officer in direct control of the entire contingent in the Low Countries. Under the duke's studious guidance the disparate elements of the Allied Army were organized into three corps and a reserve. The Hereditary Prince of Orange-Nassau was given the command of the 1st Corps, and his headquarters established in Braine-le-Comte; Lieutenant-General Rowland, Lord Hill commanded the 2nd Corps from the headquarters in Grammont; the British and Hanoverian cavalry and horse artillery were combined into one command under the Earl of Uxbridge, and were massed along both banks of the Dendre River, with the headquarters at Ninove; and the reserve, which consisted of a variety of troops, was in the immediate vicinity of Brussels, nominally under the Duke of Wellington's personal supervision. This wide disposition was dictated by the necessity to safeguard the ports of Antwerp and Ostend. Accordingly, outposts were established on the frontier, notably at Mons, to ensure that any enemy movements in this direction were reported.

The Duke of Wellington and Feldmarschall Blücher believed that their combined forces were strong enough to repel a French attack, and by the middle of June the duke in particular gave little credence to the intelligence being supplied by the outpost at Mons that the French had massed more than 100,000 men on the frontier between Maubeuge and Philippeville for an invasion. Indeed, his thoughts turned to the mundane, of renumbering various parts of the army, and the elevation of the Duke of Brunswick to the command of the reserve. Events were set to determine otherwise.

CHRONOLOGY

1815

26 February
Napoleon escapes exile on the island of Elba with his tiny body of men and sails with a small flotilla to France.

1 March
The former emperor lands on the coast at Golfe Juan, but having failed to gain Antibes marches towards Grasse.

7 March
News of Napoleon's escape and subsequent return to France reaches the delegates at the Congress of Vienna.

11 March
In Brussels the residents learn of Napoleon's return to France, as émigrés cross the border into the Low Countries.

17 March
The Sovereign Prince is proclaimed King Willem I of the United Netherlands, and his eldest son is declared the Hereditary Prince of Orange-Nassau.

4 April
The Duke of Wellington arrives in Brussels and establishes his headquarters on the rue Royale.

11 April
Wellington issues a General Order and assumes the command of all the British and Hanoverian troops.

5 May
The Armée du Nord is officially formed and the concentration on the border with the Low Countries increases.

7 May
King Willem I issues a decree appointing the Duke of Wellington Field Marshal of the Netherlands Army.

1 June
Deputations gather in Paris for the Champ de Mai, the state occasion at which Napoleon amends the civil code and presents new Eagles to the French Army.

12 June
Napoleon leaves Paris in the early hours of the morning for the frontier, and arrives in the evening at Laon.

14 June
The emperor reaches Beaumont and from Imperial Headquarters issues orders of movement to the French Army.

15 June

3:00am
The left wing of the French Army crosses the Sambre River and comes into contact with the Prussian outposts at Lobbes and Thuin.

5:00am
The Hereditary Prince of Orange-Nassau visits St Symphorien. But finding everything quiet he returns to Braine-le-Comte and then departs for Brussels.

11:00am	Charleroi is captured by the French. Napoleon orders Maréchal Grouchy and Comte Vandamme to take the Sombreffe road to Fleurus, while Comte Reille marches north towards Brussels.
Midday	Baron Constant-Rebècque at Braine-le-Comte receives news from Mons that the Prussians have been attacked, and forwards the communication to Brussels.
3:00pm	The Prince of Orange-Nassau informs the Duke of Wellington of his intelligence while they are at dinner. This is corroborated by the Prussian liaison officer, Freiherr von Müffling.
3:30pm	Maréchal Ney and his aide-de-camp arrive at Charleroi, and to his surprise Napoleon appoints him to the command of the left wing of the French Army.
6:00pm	The French engage the Prussian rearguard at Gilly, and following a fierce action the Prussians retire towards Sombreffe.
	The Lanciers Rouges of the Garde Impériale attack the Allied outpost at Frasnes, forcing the Nassau troops stationed there to retire to the crossroads at Quatre Bras.
	In Brussels the Duke of Wellington issues orders for the Allied troops to assemble at their respective headquarters.
8:00pm	The 2nd Netherlands Division concentrates at Quatre Bras, and Baron Perponcher-Sedlnitsky sends word of the engagement to Baron Constant-Rebècque at Braine-le-Comte.
10:00pm	Baron Constant-Rebècque is informed of the French advance and shortly thereafter he receives Wellington's orders, which he disregards. He sends Lieutenant Henry Webster to Brussels with details of the true state of affairs.
11:30pm	The Duke of Wellington receives confirmation from the outpost at Mons of the French attack, and issues supplementary orders to the Allied Army. He and his staff then attend a ball being given by the Duchess of Richmond.
Midnight	Henry Webster arrives in the capital before midnight, and makes his way to the Duke and Duchess of Richmond's residence. Here he delivers the news of the French attack upon Quatre Bras to the Duke of Wellington.

16 June

3:30am	The Hereditary Prince of Orange-Nassau returns to Braine-le-Comte and, accompanied by Baron Constant-Rebècque, rides to Quatre Bras.
4:00am	Napoleon rises at Imperial Headquarters in Charleroi and issues orders to Maréchal Ney at Gosselies.
8:00am	The Duke of Wellington and his staff ride out of Brussels for the front, stopping at the farm of Mont St Jean en route.
8:30am	Napoleon dictates a detailed letter to Maréchal Ney, and another shortly thereafter to Maréchal Grouchy, explaining his plans for the forthcoming campaign. He then travels to Fleurus.

10:00am	The Duke of Wellington and his party arrive at Quatre Bras, but finding everything quiet he rides to the windmill of Bussy at Brye to meet with Feldmarschall Blücher.
11:00am	Comte de Flahaut reaches Frasnes with the emperor's letter for Maréchal Ney. The skirmishing between the outposts gradually increases.
2:00pm	The French commence the attack upon Quatre Bras as Baron Bachelu and Comte Foy's divisions, supported by the cavalry led by Comte Piré, advance.
	Napoleon writes to Ney from Fleurus, informing him of the action at Sombreffe, and ordering him to envelope the right flank of the Prussian Army.
2:30pm	Gémioncourt is captured by the troops of Baron Jamin's Brigade and the Dutch defending the centre are driven back.
3:00pm	The Duke of Wellington returns to Quatre Bras as the vanguard from Sir Thomas Picton's 5th Division arrives at the crossroads.
3:15pm	Napoleon commences the attack upon the villages of Ligny and St Amand and writes to Ney again, ordering him to manoeuvre to the heights of Brye and St Amand.
3:30pm	The Dutch and Belgian cavalry under Baron van Merlen engage the French cavalry and are forced to retreat in disorder. The guns at the crossroads are overrun.
3:45pm	Sir Thomas Picton attacks the French on the left of the Allied line with the 5th Division.
	At Fleurus, Napoleon writes to Comte d'Erlon, directing him to the heights of St Amand with the entire I Corps.
4:00pm	The majority of the Brunswick Corps reaches the battlefield and the troops are immediately thrown into the action.
	Jérôme Bonaparte's 6th Division arrives and is personally led by Maréchal Ney towards the Bois de Bossu.
4:15pm	The Duke of Brunswick is mortally wounded and carried back to the crossroads. The command of the Brunswick Corps devolves upon Colonel Olfermann.
4:30pm	A concerted attack is launched upon the centre of the Allied line by the French cavalry and the two battalions of the 3e Régiment de Ligne.
	During the engagement John Cameron of the 92nd Regiment of Foot is mortally wounded.
4:45pm	The *chasseurs* and *lanciers* belonging to Comte Piré's Cavalry Division attack the Allied troops defending the centre of the line.
5:00pm	Count Alten arrives with the 3rd Division. The troops of Halkett's Brigade deploy adjacent to the Bois de Bossu.
	Comte d'Erlon receives Napoleon's order and marches towards St Amand, while the emperor's second order is delivered to Ney, who calls for Comte d'Erlon to advance to Quatre Bras.

5:15pm	The Hanoverian troops of Count Kielmansegge's Brigade attack Piraumont and drive the French out of the hamlet.
5:30pm	Maréchal Ney is informed that Comte d'Erlon has marched with I Corps to St Amand, and so he orders the *cuirassiers* from Comte Valmy's III Reserve Cavalry Corps to charge.
5:45pm	The *cuirassiers* attack the Allied formations and capture the King's Colour of the 69th Regiment of Foot. However, they suffer severe losses during the charge and are forced to retire.
6:00pm	Major-General Cooke arrives at the head of the 1st Division and the Hereditary Prince of Orange-Nassau directs the 1st Brigade into the Bois de Bossu.
6:30pm	The British Foot Guards drive the French out of the wood and debouch to the south, but they are assailed by heavy artillery fire and forced to retire into the heart of the Bois de Bossu.
	Comte d'Erlon arrives with I Corps opposite Wagnelée and causes consternation in the French Army already engaged at St Amand. The commander of the corps is informed of the situation at Quatre Bras and decides to return with the majority of his men.
6:45pm	The remnants of the *chasseurs* and *lanciers* under Comte Pirè attack the Allied squares in the centre of the line.
7:00pm	Seconde-Lieutenant von Wussow of the Prussian General Staff arrives at Quatre Bras with a message for the Duke of Wellington from Graf Neidhardt von Gneisenau, who requests the duke to attack the enemy immediately.
7:15pm	Wellington instructs the Brunswick troops to advance on the right of the Allied line, close to the Bois de Bossu. The Hanoverians at Piraumont also attack the French.
7:30pm	The British Foot Guards debouch the Bois de Bossu, but are attacked by the French cavalry and sustain very heavy losses.
8:00pm	Major-General Dörnberg arrives at the crossroads with the first of the British cavalry, and pushes the 23rd Light Dragoons forward into the front line.
8:30pm	Gémioncourt is recaptured by the Allied troops as the French slowly withdraw from their positions.
9:00pm	The fighting at Quatre Bras gradually subsides, and outposts are deployed along the Allied line. Wellington and his staff retire to his headquarters in Genappe. The Prince of Orange-Nassau also leaves the field, returning to Nivelles.
	Comte d'Erlon reaches Frasnes with the vanguard of the I Corps and these troops replace those of the II Corps. He is called to a meeting with Maréchal Ney at Gosselies.
10:00pm	Ney writes a short report of events to Maréchal Soult, Napoleon's chief of staff, and awaits further instructions from the emperor.
	The French defeat the Prussians at Ligny and St Amand, but the onset of night prevents them from pursuing, and so the victory is not conclusive. Napoleon is at Fleurus, unaware of the outcome of the fighting at Quatre Bras.

OPPOSING COMMANDERS

No campaign in the history of military conflict has evoked greater debate or scrutiny than Waterloo. One of the principal reasons for this ardent interest is the brilliance of the opposing commanders and the notoriety of their immediate subordinates, for it was their decisions that governed the various armies in the field and shaped the dramatic course of events. This is also one of the fundamental points of issue when examining the campaign, because Waterloo was more than a series of battles and the commanders were more than mere generals. They were statesmen versed in the politics of the day, and the military operations they prescribed were dictated in great part by social and political circumstances.

While the commanders carried the burden of expectation, not only of their soldiers but of their respective nations, their immediate subordinates were charged with the impossible task of walking in their shadow. This ultimately proved injurious, for it was they who suffered the greatest injustice in the aftermath of the campaign.

ALLIED COMMANDERS

Sir Arthur Wellesley, 1st Duke of Wellington
At the time of his arrival in the Low Countries Wellington bore the hallmarks of a man destined for high office. He had attained a reputation as a formidable military tactician and was a politician of considerable stature.

Born on 1 May 1769, Wellesley was the third surviving son of Garret, 1st Earl of Mornington, an Anglo-Irish Peer who died when Arthur was a boy. An unremarkable education at Eton had been followed by attendance at the academy in Angers, where he learned to speak fluent French. But he was not an aspiring academic, and so he resorted to the usual expedient of the day and obtained a commission in the British Army. Judicious use of the purchase system enabled him to rise rapidly through the ranks, serving in both infantry and cavalry regiments, and by the end of 1793 he was a lieutenant-colonel in the 33rd Regiment of Foot.

It was now that Wellesley experienced active service as part of the army commanded by the Duke of York in Flanders. Unfortunately, this proved thoroughly chastening and, having failed to obtain civil employment, he was subsequently posted to India where his elder brother was governor general. The benefits he received due to his brother's position were manifest, but it was here that he developed the many qualities he would later exhibit on the

Sir Arthur Wellesley, 1st Duke of Wellington, commanded the Allied Army stationed in the Low Countries. He was a formidable military tactician who attained the trust and respect of his troops. Painting by Sir Thomas Lawrence. (Apsley House, The Wellington Museum, London, UK / Bridgeman Images)

battlefields of Europe. He was knighted upon his return to England in 1805, but spent four years in mainly administrative roles before being given the chance to demonstrate his prowess as a leader in the Iberian Peninsula.

Between 1809 and 1814 he achieved a string of notable victories against the French forces in Portugal, Spain and France which elevated him to the rank of field marshal and secured the title 1st Duke of Wellington. The financial rewards were also very substantial. With Napoleon exiled to Elba, he was appointed ambassador to the court of the restored Bourbon King, Louis XVIII, where his ability to engender excellent relations with the French monarch indicated that he was ideally suited to replace Viscount Castlereagh as the British plenipotentiary at the Congress of Vienna, when the former returned to England in February 1815.

The Duke of Wellington was aloof and abrasive, but he had an undeniable respect for the lives of his soldiers which earned him their trust, and this would bode well for the hard fighting ahead.

Willem, Hereditary Prince of Orange-Nassau

Despite being only 22 years of age, Willem was an experienced officer who had served with the British Army during the Peninsular War. Engaging and well liked, he fulfilled his military duties capably.

Born on 6 December 1792, he was the eldest son of Willem, the future king of the United Netherlands. When the French overran Holland in 1794, the young prince fled with his family to Berlin. It was here that his maternal grandfather, King Friedrich Wilhelm II of Prussia, appointed Baron Jean-Victor de Constant-Rebècque as his military governor, and in 1805 Willem entered the Military Academy. He was an excellent student, graduating with distinction in 1809, and was commissioned in the Prussian Army with the rank of Lieutenant. However, in May he left Berlin with Baron Constant-Rebècque in order to further his education in England, where he attended Oxford University. Having achieved a doctorate in law, in 1811 he joined the British Army, and with the rank of lieutenant-colonel he departed for Portugal along with Baron Constant-Rebècque, for service in Spain.

Upon his arrival the prince was appointed aide-de-camp to the Duke of Wellington. In September that year he distinguished himself during the fighting at El Bodon, and in October was promoted to the rank of colonel. He remained with the British Army throughout 1812, and was present during the storming of St Francisco, Ciudad Rodrigo and Badajoz. He was rebuked for his conduct at Ciudad Rodrigo, because he had personally joined the attack upon the redoubt. That year he participated in the battle at Salamanca, the siege of Burgos and the capture of Madrid. Indeed, he was rewarded for his part in taking the castle at Retiro by being appointed adjutant to the Prince Regent.

The young prince maintained his distinguished service record in 1813, being present at the battle of Vitoria and the siege of St Sebastian. He served in the actions in the Pyrenees, and on 5 August the Duke of Wellington sent him to England with the dispatches. While in London his father was recognized by the British government as the Sovereign Prince, and on 13 December, he was promoted to major-general in the British Army. He subsequently returned to his homeland and during the war of liberation against the French was made Commander-in-Chief of the Dutch Army. He succeeded Sir Thomas Graham in the summer of 1814 as Commander of the British Subsidiary Army in the Netherlands, being promoted to lieutenant-general, and then full general almost immediately thereafter. He held this position until the arrival of the Duke of Wellington.

His personal bravery was never disputed, and his diligent service allowed Wellington to command the numerous Dutch and Belgian troops serving with the Allied Army in a manner the duke believed most advisable.

Willem Frederik Lodewijk Georges, the Hereditary Prince of Orange-Nassau, served diligently in the British Army during the Peninsular War and in 1815 commanded I Corps of the Allied Army. Painting by François Josephe. (The Bowes Museum, Barnard Castle, County Durham, UK / Bridgeman Images)

FRENCH COMMANDERS

Napoleon Bonaparte, Emperor of France

Of all those who rose to prominence from the wellspring of the Revolution, none was able to impose their will upon the people of France like Napoleon. He was a ruthless opportunist with an insatiable lust for power.

Born on 15 August 1769, he was the third surviving son of Carlo Bonaparte, a wealthy lawyer of Corsican nobility. Having obtained a scholarship at the French Military Academy in Brienne-le-Château, he embarked upon a career of unparalleled success. An avid student, reading history, law and philosophy, after graduating from the École Militaire in Paris he was commissioned into the Régiment de la Fère. It was here that Napoleon developed an overriding belief in the power of artillery, which he demonstrated in 1795 during the royalist uprising in Paris. This act brought him to the attention of the National Convention and earned him promotion to Commander of the Armée d'Italie.

He now commenced the first of many campaigns in which he elevated strategy to an art form. The unrivalled success he gained over the Habsburg and Piedmont armies secured political influence and considerable wealth. It also persuaded him to fund an ill-fated expedition to Egypt, during which he sought further glory. His ambitions knew no bounds, and in 1799 he participated in the Coup d'Brumaire in order to overthrow the unpopular

Napoleon Bonaparte, Emperor of France, recognized the hostility of the sovereigns and the strength of the coalition force united against him in 1815, but was convinced of his own infallibility. Painting by unknown artist. (Musée de la Légion d'Honneur, Paris / René Chartrand)

government. Napoleon assumed the position of Premier Consul, but within months had ousted those with whom he shared power and established himself as the leader of France. This was confirmed in 1804 when Pope Pius VII crowned Napoleon emperor, and he created the *maréchalat*.

The sovereigns of Europe were united against France. Austria and Russia formed a coalition, but Napoleon defeated their armies at Ulm and Austerlitz in 1805, and a year later inflicted a crushing defeat on the Prussians at Jena-Auerstädt which forced them to sue for peace. His ability to inspire devotion and loyalty among his troops on the battlefield was extraordinary, which together with the rapid movement of his army enabled him to envelop opposing forces in a manner that was unheralded. However, his maniacal desire to create a Bonaparte dynasty encouraged the sovereigns to rise again, and the tide turned. The invasion of Russia in 1812 was a disaster. The Grande Armée was almost annihilated during the retreat from Moscow that winter, and never recovered. Napoleon was subsequently defeated at Leipzig in 1813, and forced to withdraw to the haven of France, where he fought a string of successful battles. But his position as head of state and commander of the army had been weakened and the marshals demanded his abdication. Napoleon went into exile on the tiny island of Elba, only to return within a year and plunge Europe into turmoil once more.

At the beginning of the campaign he was suffering with a variety of physical ailments which muted his performance. Yet Napoleon was convinced of his own infallibility and that the outcome would be favourable.

Michel Ney, Prince de la Moskowa

Ney was the son of a lowly barrel cooper who rose from the chaos of the Revolution to become a *maréchal* of France. A courageous leader with a violent temper, he placed the welfare of the nation above his personal glory.

Born on 10 January 1769, he was the second surviving son of Pierre Ney, who had fought in the ranks during the Seven Years War. Michel was educated by monks at the Collège des Augustins, and spoke French and German. He was subsequently apprenticed to a lawyer, but he ran away and enlisted in the Régiment des Hussards de Colonel-général. Ney fought his first action in 1792, and four years later had risen to the rank of Général de Brigade. He commanded a number of cavalry units against the Austrians at the battle of Neuwied, and conducted the operations of a sizeable body of cavalry in Switzerland.

In 1799 he was promoted to the command of a division and was required to perform various diplomatic duties, which he did with poise. But he had no appetite for the vagaries of politics or statesmen. Ney was accustomed to the hardship of a soldier's life, and was surprised to be summoned to the ceremony and splendour of the Tuileries in 1801. It was here that he met Napoleon, who recognized a kindred spirit and made him an integral part of the Consulate. Upon crowning himself emperor Napoleon created the *maréchalat*, and immediately elevated Ney to the highest military rank.

Michel Ney, Prince de la Moskowa, was appointed to the command of the left wing of the army, and led the French force at Quatre Bras with his customary vigour. Painting by François-Pascal Gérard. (Musée de l'Armée, Paris / René Chartrand)

Ney served the empire with distinction, participating in the battles of Jena, Eylau and Friedland, earning the title Duc d'Elchingen. In 1808 he was sent to Spain, but his fiery temperament proved divisive. Ney quarrelled with Maréchal André Masséna, his immediate superior, and was ordered to return to France. He was redeemed during the disastrous retreat from Moscow in the winter of 1812, when he commanded the rearguard with such bravery and resourcefulness that the emperor bestowed upon him the title Prince de la Moskowa.

The campaigns of 1813 and 1814 saw the war reach French soil and as the coalition forces advanced towards Paris, Ney demanded Napoleon's abdication. When Paris fell he pledged his allegiance to the restored Bourbon king, which enabled him to retain his land and titles. But his humble origins prevented Ney from being accepted by the monarchy, until news arrived of Napoleon's return from Elba. At this moment the king and his followers placed their faith in his ability to command the army. Ney was tormented by the prospect of civil war, and vowed to thwart his former master at Bésançon. But when he arrived the garrison openly displayed their contempt for the king and their desire to embrace Napoleon. Having been solicited to meet the former emperor at Chalon-sur-Saône, Ney announced his support for Napoleon, and with this decision the king lost his realm.

By June 1815 Ney exhibited the scars of a hundred battles. The fire which had once marked his devotion to France had been eroded, but he still enjoyed the adulation of the army and his companions in arms.

OPPOSING FORCES

The opposing commanders led forces of vastly different calibre into the field at the beginning of the campaign. While the French Army was for the most part composed of seasoned troops, the Allied Army commanded by the Duke of Wellington was an inexperienced collection of British, Hanoverian, Brunswick and Nassau contingents, augmented by newly formed units from the United Netherlands consisting of Dutch and Belgians. Many of the veteran British soldiers that Wellington had honed into a dependable fighting force during the Peninsular War had been sent to North America, and so a considerable proportion of those to arrive in the Low Countries were

untried. Fortunately, the duke could also call upon the officers and men of the King's German Legion. Predominately Hanoverian, they had distinguished themselves on a number of occasions in the British Army, having volunteered for service following the French occupation of Hanover in 1803. These were judiciously mixed with the Hanoverian Light Infantry and *Landwehr* (militia) battalions, and along with the British they formed a core upon which Wellington relied.

The duke was concerned by the loyalty of the Dutch and Belgian troops, a sentiment borne out of the fact that many of the officers and men had served within the French Army. This prevailed to such an extent that he refrained from liaising with their senior officers outside of social events, preferring instead to correspond exclusively through the Hereditary Prince of Orange-Nassau. Although prudent, this endangered the lines of communication available to the general headquarters in Brussels in the event of a French attack.

THE COMMAND AND COMPOSITION OF THE ALLIED ARMY

Upon his arrival in the Low Countries the Duke of Wellington encountered a number of obstacles, not least the low number of troops he was expected to command in the forthcoming campaign. He immediately wrote to Earl Bathurst, the Secretary for War and the Colonies, about the strength of the force at his disposal and called upon Parliament to deliver the 60,000 men which had been stipulated as the minimum British contingent by the Treaty of Chaumont.

Despite the many issues with the rank and file, the duke managed to secure the vast majority of the officers he requested for the general staff. Lord Fitzroy Somerset resumed the role of Military Secretary, and lieutenant-colonels John Fremantle, Charles Canning and the Hon Sir Alexander Gordon were reappointed as his aides-de-camp. Sir Edward Barnes was the Adjutant-General; Colonel Sir George Wood commanded the artillery, with Lieutenant-Colonel Sir Augustus Frazer in charge of the Royal Horse Artillery, while the engineers were under the direction of Sir James Carmichael-Smyth. The post of Quartermaster-General was filled by Sir George Murray. However, as he was serving with the British force in Canada, in the interim the role was undertaken by Sir William Howe de Lancey, the Deputy Quartermaster-General. The Duke of Wellington sought to obtain the services of Lord Combermere, who had commanded the British cavalry in the Peninsula, but at the express wish of the Prince Regent the command was given to Lieutenant-General Henry Paget, the Earl of Uxbridge.

With the general staff established, the duke organized the army into three corps and a reserve. The Hereditary Prince of Orange-Nassau was given the command of the 1st Corps; Lieutenant-General Rowland, Lord Hill commanded the 2nd Corps; the British and Hanoverian cavalry and horse artillery were combined into one command under the Earl of Uxbridge; while the reserve, which consisted of a variety of troops, was in the vicinity of Brussels.

The 1st Corps was composed of four infantry divisions and a division of cavalry, each of which was supplemented by batteries of artillery. The 1st Division, commanded by Major-General George Cooke, had its headquarters in Enghien; the 3rd Division, under Lieutenant-General Count Carl von Alten, had its headquarters in Soignies; the 2nd Netherlands Division was under the command of Lieutenant-General Baron Henri-Georges de Perponcher-Sedlnitsky, with the headquarters in Nivelles; the 3rd Netherlands Division, under Lieutenant-General Baron David-Henri Chassé, had its headquarters in Haine St Pierre, between Mons and Binche; the Netherlands Cavalry Division, commanded by Lieutenant-General Baron Jean-Marie de Collaert, had its headquarters in Boussoit-sur-Haine, to the east of Mons, with the troops in cantonments in the intervening towns and villages. Major-General Baron Jean-Victor de Constant-Rebècque fulfilled the role of quartermaster-general or chief of staff to the Hereditary Prince of Orange-Nassau, and was situated in the headquarters at the Hôtel du Miroir in Braine-le-Comte.

One of a lengthy series of illustrations executed during the occupation of Paris in the aftermath of the campaign. This shows a Dutch militiaman wearing a number of items supplied by the British. Print by Genty. (Bibliothèque Nationale de France, Paris / René Chartrand)

Carl von Alten was a distinguished Hanoverian officer who served in the British Army throughout the Peninsular War. He commanded the troops in the 3rd British Division during the campaign. Miniature by François Rochard. (Historisches Museum, Hanover)

Baron Constant-Rebècque was a Swiss of French ancestry. Like many Swiss, he had served in a number of different European armies against Napoleon. During service in the Prussian Army he became acquainted with Willem, the future Hereditary Prince of Orange-Nassau, whom he tutored in the art of military science. He accompanied him throughout his service with the British Army in the Iberian Peninsula, and following the creation of the United Netherlands, played a prominent part in the organization of the new army and the initial plans for the defence of the realm.

George Cooke had the honour of commanding the 1st Division, composed of four battalions of British Foot Guards. He was an experienced officer who had served in a number of capacities. Having attained his captaincy in the 1st Guards he was sent to Flanders in 1794, where he was appointed aide-de-camp to Major-General Sir Samuel Hulse. He participated in the expedition to the Scheldt and commanded the garrison at Cadiz, before returning to Belgium at the end of 1813.

The 3rd Division comprised three large brigades and was commanded by Count Carl von Alten, a distinguished Hanoverian officer who had participated in the early years of the Revolutionary Wars. When Hanover was invaded and the army disbanded, he volunteered for the King's German Legion. He served throughout the Peninsular War, eventually being placed at the head of the Light Division, and was widely respected by his fellow officers and the rank and file.

Sir Thomas Picton was appointed to the command of the 5th British Division in 1815. A courageous Welshman with a fiery temperament, he had endured political censure for his governorship of Trinidad, but overcame this to play an important role within the British Army. Painting by Sir William Beechey. (Apsley House, The Wellington Museum, London, UK / Bridgeman Images)

Each of these divisions was supported by the reserve, under the Duke of Wellington's immediate direction. At the beginning of June this comprised the 5th and 6th British divisions, and the Brunswick Corps. Sir Thomas Picton commanded the 5th, which was composed of veteran British troops, including a number of the famed Highland regiments, and the 6th Division in the absence of

Lieutenant-General Sir Galbraith Lowry Cole. Despite a chequered political career, Picton had proven his qualities in the Peninsula when leading the 3rd Division of Wellington's army and the duke had requested the courageous Welshman for service in the Low Countries. However, Picton's health had deteriorated and he was tired of campaigning, so he stipulated that he would leave his estate in Pembrokeshire on condition that he received orders only from the Duke of Wellington.

Another inveterate enemy of France was Friedrich Wilhelm, the Duke of Brunswick. Following the death of his father at the battle of Auerstädt in 1806, the young duke had taken arms against the French, but after a series of reversals in mainland Europe he fled to England. Here he reorganized the corps of troops he had raised and joined the British in the Peninsular War. The Brunswick troops acquitted themselves well, so when Napoleon returned to power in France the Duke of Brunswick agreed to raise a new corps for service alongside the British, although most of those he brought to the Low Countries were young and inexperienced.

On 7 June the three battalions of the 1st Nassau-Usingen Regiment, under the command of Major-General Baron August von Kruse, arrived in the Low Countries. They were quartered in the vicinity of Brussels as part of the reserve, along with the 5th and 6th divisions and the Brunswick Corps. Their comrades serving in the three battalions of the 2nd Nassau-Usingen Regiment and the 1st Battalion Orange-Nassau had been stationed in the Low Countries since 1814 as part of the United Netherlands Army, and formed a brigade within the 2nd Netherlands Division under Baron Perponcher-Sedlnitsky. The troops were deployed in Houtain-le-Val, Frasnes, Genappe and the surrounding area. On 12 June they were joined by the 2nd Battalion 28th Orange-Nassau, and a company of volunteer *Jäger*. With the arrival of the Nassau the Allied Army numbered almost 112,000 men, with 204 pieces of artillery. The Prussian Army was larger still, approaching 127,000 men, with 304 guns. Consequently, the Duke of Wellington and Feldmarschall Blücher believed that their respective forces were sufficient to take the offensive and advance into France along with the other coalition armies.

THE COMMAND AND COMPOSITION OF THE FRENCH ARMY

Having regained the throne, Napoleon attempted to unite the French nation and to safeguard his regime. He appointed the most loyal of his marshals, Louis-Nicolas Davout, as the Minister for War, and immediately wrote to the various government departments about the reimplementation of the imperial constitution. However, the emperor knew that a great deal would depend on the continued allegiance of the army and that the fidelity of the senior officers was paramount to the morale of the troops. When he wrote to Maréchal Davout at the end of March with details of the contingents to garrison the frontier fortresses, he duly specified the most dependable of his generals for the command posts.

Napoleon recognized the hostility of the Allied sovereigns and the immense force which had been put in motion towards the French borders, yet he hoped to dissolve the coalition with a single victory. He determined to take the offensive and fall upon the Allied and Prussian armies stationed in the Low Countries. The chain of fortresses on the northern frontier would veil the concentration of the army, and he would direct operations personally. However, the turbulent political climate in France rendered it necessary to gain support before the commencement of hostilities. Consequently, Napoleon embarked upon a programme of reform. An amendment to the constitution was proposed whereby the emperor would exercise legislative power in concurrence with the hereditary Chamber of Peers and the elected Chamber of Deputies. The right of petition and the freedom of worship were recognized, and slavery was abolished. The levy of men for the army could only be granted by law, and no part of France could be placed in a state of siege except in the case of foreign invasion or civil unrest. The act also declared that the nation would not consent to the reinstatement of the Bourbons, or of any prince of that family on the throne, even in the case of the extinction of the imperial dynasty. All of these measures were to be added to the constitution in the solemn ceremony of the Champ de Mai, which would be attended by delegations from the Electoral Colleges and the military.

By the end of April Napoleon had introduced measures to recruit, arm and equip an army to meet the coalition forces, and the general aspect of the country was warlike. Thereafter, he turned his attention to the composition and command structure of the army destined to take the field in the forthcoming campaign. The Armée du Nord was composed of I, II, III, IV and VI Corps under Comtes d'Erlon, Reille, Vandamme, Gérard and Lobau respectively. Four corps of reserve cavalry were led by Maréchal Emmanuel-Henri, Marquis de Grouchy, while Maréchal Édouard-Adolphe Mortier assumed his customary position at the head of the Garde Impériale. The post of major-général or chief of staff, with the responsibility of coordinating the movements of the entire French Army, was filled by Maréchal Nicolas-Jean de Dieu Soult.

Jean-Baptiste Drouet, Comte d'Erlon, was one of several officers who attempted to support Napoleon when he returned to France in March 1815. He was rewarded for his loyalty with command of I Corps. Painting by Ary Scheffer. (Musee des Beaux-Arts, Reims, France / Roger-Viollet, Paris / Bridgeman Images)

Jean-Baptiste Drouet, Comte d'Erlon, was rewarded for his loyalty with the command of I Corps. A vastly experienced soldier, he had served with distinction in both the Revolutionary and Imperial armies. Having risen through the ranks, he played a vital role as a divisional commander at the battle of Austerlitz, and was present at all the major actions of the period, including Jena and Friedland. He enjoyed considerable success with each of his subsequent commands, and remained a devoted advocate of the emperor following his abdication.

The I Corps was composed of four divisions of infantry and a division of cavalry. The 1st Division was initially commanded by Jacques-Alexandre, Comte Allix de Vaux, but he was sent to Lyon prior to the start of the campaign, and so the command devolved upon Baron Joachim-Jérôme Quiot de Passage; the 2nd Division was led by Baron François-Xavier Donzelot; the 3rd was commanded by Baron Pierre-Louis Binet de Marcognet and the 4th by Joseph-François, Comte Durutte; the 1st Cavalry Division was under the command of Baron Charles-Claude Jacquinot. In addition to these divisions there was a sizeable reserve artillery and contingent of engineers.

Honoré-Charles, Comte Reille, had enjoyed modest success against the British and their allies in the Iberian Peninsula, and subsequently adopted a cautious approach during the engagement at Quatre Bras. Coloured engraving after Maurin. (Author's collection)

Honoré-Charles, Comte Reille, was appointed to the command of II Corps. A veteran who had served in the early campaigns of the Revolutionary Wars, by 1805 he had been promoted to command of a brigade, and served as aide-de-camp to Napoleon at the battle of Friedland. He enjoyed modest success against the British and their allies in the Iberian Peninsula, being defeated at the battle of Vitoria, and like many of his fellow officers, had accepted a position in the French Army during the brief Bourbon reign. But he rallied to the emperor upon his return to France.

The II Corps was also composed of four divisions of infantry and one of cavalry. The 5th Division was led by Baron Gilbert-Désirée Bachelu; the 6th by Jérôme Bonaparte, the emperor's younger brother, who was supported in this role by the vast experience of his second-in-command, Armand-Charles, Comte Guilleminot; the 7th was led by Baron Jean-Baptiste Girard, while the 9th was under Maximilien-Sébastien, Comte Foy. The 2nd Cavalry Division was commanded by Hippolyte-Marie, Comte Piré. As with each of the French Army corps, these divisions were supplemented by reserve artillery and a considerable body of engineers.

At the outset of the campaign the cadre and quality of the officers and men within the various Régiments de Ligne was extremely high, thereby ensuring the infantry was well disciplined. Print by Martinet. (Bibliothèque Nationale de France, Paris)

On 1 June the deputations gathered in Paris for the ceremony of the Champ de Mai. It was a glorious state occasion at which Napoleon amended the civil code and presented new Eagles to the army. The spectacle marked the beginning of the escalation for war, and at the conclusion the troops returned to their respective regiments. The concentration of the strike force on the northern frontier continued, but the recruitment of men was insufficient to meet the requirements of the whole army, and so Napoleon turned to conscription. Under the terms of the amended constitution, the power to conscript lay solely with the Chamber of Deputies, and following an initial rejection the emperor succeeded in calling the levy of 1814, which had not been called in his absence by the Bourbons. The conscripts released experienced soldiers from the garrisons, and these joined the various corps stationed around Beaumont.

Situation with all three armies, the night of 14–15 June 1815

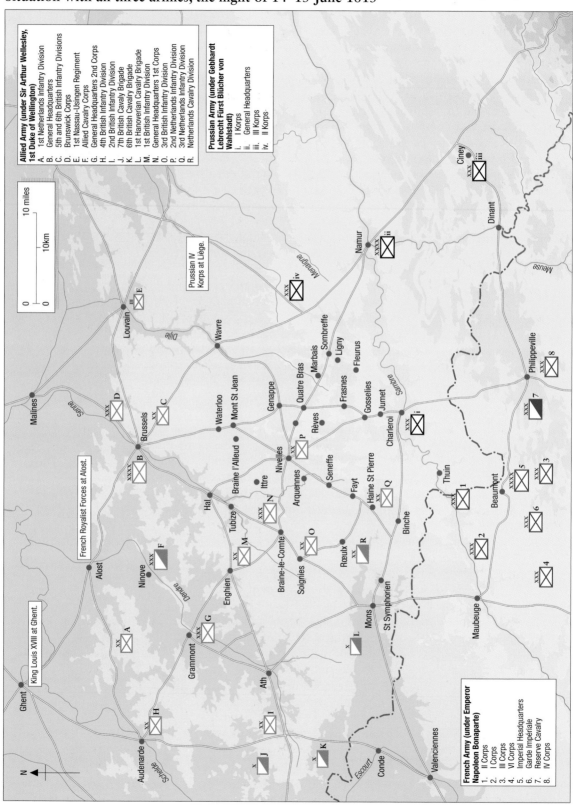

Allied Army (under Sir Arthur Wellesley, 1st Duke of Wellington)
A. 1st Netherlands Infantry Division
B. General Headquarters
C. 5th and 6th British Infantry Divisions
D. Brunswick Corps
E. 1st Nassau–Usingen Regiment
F. Allied Cavalry Corps
G. General Headquarters 2nd Corps
H. 4th British Infantry Division
I. 2nd British Infantry Division
J. 7th British Cavaly Brigade
K. 6th British Cavalry Brigade
L. 1st Hanoverian Cavalry Brigade
M. 1st British Infantry Division
N. General Headquarters 1st Corps
O. 3rd British Infantry Division
P. 2nd Netherlands Infantry Division
Q. 3rd Netherlands Infantry Division
R. Netherlands Cavalry Division

Prussian Army (under Gebhardt Lebrecht Fürst Blücher von Wahlstadt)
i. I Korps
ii. General Headquarters
iii. III Korps
iv. II Korps·

French Army (under Emperor Napoleon Bonaparte)
1. II Corps
2. I Corps
3. III Corps
4. VI Corps
5. Imperial Headquarters
6. Garde Impériale
7. Reserve Cavalry
8. IV Corps

Prussian IV Korps at Liège.

French Royalist Forces at Alost.

King Louis XVIII at Ghent.

10 miles

10km

Napoleon left Paris in the early hours of 12 June and travelled by carriage to Laon, where he spent the night. He was aware that the force at his disposal was approaching 130,000 men of all arms, with 358 guns, and that Maréchal Mortier had asked to be excused service in the campaign as he had been struck down by a severe attack of sciatica. The following morning the emperor continued to Avesnes and breakfasted with Maréchal Ney, who had received instructions from the Minister for War to join him. On the 14th Napoleon removed to Beaumont, where his headquarters were established at the Château des Caraman-Chimay, and with his customary zeal Napoleon dictated elaborate orders to Maréchal Soult for the movement of the army.

The final preparations having been completed, the campfires were extinguished and the troops moved slowly from their bivouacs to the designated assembly points, animated by their devotion to the emperor and the full confidence of victory.

The French Army never recovered from the losses it sustained during the disastrous retreat from Moscow, but by 1815 there were sufficient horses to ensure that this arm made a substantial contribution. Print by Martinet. (Bibliothèque Nationale de France, Paris)

ORDERS OF BATTLE

ALLIED FORCES AT QUATRE BRAS

Commander-in-Chief: Field Marshal Sir Arthur Wellesley, Duke of Wellington
Military Secretary: Lieutenant-Colonel Lord Fitzroy Somerset
Commanding Royal Artillery: Colonel Sir George Wood
Commanding Royal Horse Artillery: Lieutenant-Colonel Sir Augustus Frazer
Commanding KGL Artillery: Lieutenant-Colonel Sir Julius Hartmann
Commanding Royal Engineers: Lieutenant-Colonel James Carmichael-Smyth

1ST CORPS
Commanding Officer: General Willem, Hereditary Prince of Orange-Nassau
Chief of Staff: Major-General Baron Jean-Victor de Constant-Rebècque
Commanding Artillery: Major-General Carel van Gunkel
Commanding Engineers: Captain Jan Esau

2nd (Netherlands) Infantry Division
231 officers and 6,984 men
Commanding Officer: Lieutenant-General Baron Henri-Georges de Perponcher-Sedlnitsky
1st Infantry Brigade
Commanding Officer: Major-General Count Willem van Bijlandt
27th Dutch Jägers Battalion (Lieutenant-Colonel Willem Grunebosch)
7th Belgian Line Battalion (Lieutenant-Colonel François van den Sande)
5th Dutch Militia Battalion (Lieutenant-Colonel Jan Westenberg)
7th Dutch Militia Battalion (Lieutenant-Colonel Henry Singendonck)
8th Dutch Militia Battalion (Lieutenant-Colonel Wijbrandus de Jongh)
2nd Infantry Brigade
Commanding Officer: Colonel Prince Bernhard von Sachsen-Weimar
28th Orange-Nassau Regiment (Colonel Prince Bernhard von Sachsen-Weimar)
1st Battalion (Lieutenant-Colonel Wilhelm von Dressel)

2nd Battalion (Major Philip Schleijer)
2nd Nassau-Usingen Regiment (Major Johann Sattler)
1st Battalion (Captain Moritz Büsgen)
2nd Battalion (Major Philipp von Normann)
3rd Battalion (Major Gottfried Hegmann)
Volunteer Jägers (Captain Emil Bergmann)
Divisional Artillery
Belgian Foot Artillery Battery (Captain Emanuel Stevenart)
Belgian Artillery Train (Lieutenant Frederik van Gahlen)
Dutch Horse Artillery Battery (Captain Adriaan Bijleveld)
Dutch Artillery Train (Lieutenant Jacobus van der Hoeven)

Netherlands Cavalry Division
55 officers and 1,266 men
2nd Light Cavalry Brigade
Commanding Officer: Major-General Baron Jean-Baptiste van Merlen

5th Belgian Light Dragoons Regiment (Lieutenant-Colonel Édouard de Mercx)

6th Dutch Hussars Regiment (Lieutenant-Colonel Willem Boreel)

Dutch Horse Artillery (Captain Adriaan Geij)

Dutch Artillery Train (Second Lieutenant Camiese)

1st (British) Infantry Division
152 officers and 4,580 men

Commanding Officer: Major-General George Cooke

1st (British) Infantry Brigade

Commanding Officer: Major-General Peregrine Maitland

2nd Battalion 1st Regiment of Foot Guards (Colonel Henry Askew)

3rd Battalion 1st Regiment of Foot Guards (Colonel the Hon William Stuart)

2nd (British) Infantry Brigade

Commanding Officer: Major-General Sir John Byng

2nd Battalion Coldstream Regiment of Foot Guards (Colonel Alexander Woodford)

2nd Battalion 3rd Regiment of Foot Guards (Colonel Francis Hepburn)

Divisional Artillery

No 9 Company, 3rd Battalion Royal Artillery (Captain Charles Sandham)

2nd Horse Troop, King's German Legion Artillery (Brevet Major Heinrich Kuhlmann)

3rd (British) Infantry Division
265 officers and 5,819 men

Commanding Officer: Lieutenant-General Count Carl von Alten

1st (Hanoverian) Infantry Brigade

Commanding Officer: Major-General Count Friedrich von Kielmansegge

Lüneburg Light Infantry (Lieutenant-Colonel August von Klencke)

Osnabrück Light Infantry (Major Baron Carl von Bülow)

Grubenhagen Light Infantry (Lieutenant-Colonel Friedrich von Wurmb)

Verden Light Infantry (Major Julius von Schkopp)

Bremen Light Infantry (Lieutenant-Colonel Wilhelm von Langehr)

Feldjägers (Captain Christian von Reden)

5th (British) Infantry Brigade

Commanding Officer: Major-General Sir Colin Halkett

2nd Battalion 30th Regiment of Foot (Lieutenant-Colonel Alexander Hamilton)

1st Battalion 33rd Regiment of Foot (Lieutenant-Colonel William Elphinstone)

2nd Battalion 69th Regiment of Foot (Colonel Charles Morice)

2nd Battalion 73rd Regiment of Foot (Colonel William Harris)

Divisional Artillery

No 2 Company, 10th Battalion Royal Artillery (Brevet Major William Lloyd)

No 4 Company, King's German Legion Artillery (Captain Andreas Cleeves)

2ND CORPS

4th (British) Infantry Division
5 officers and 233 men

Divisional Artillery

2nd Hanoverian Foot Artillery (Captain Carl von Rettburg)

RESERVE

5th (British) Infantry Division
276 officers and 5,188 men

Commanding Officer: Lieutenant-General Sir Thomas Picton

8th (British) Infantry Brigade

Commanding Officer: Major-General Sir James Kempt

1st Battalion 28th Regiment of Foot (Lieutenant-Colonel Sir Charles Belson)

1st Battalion 32nd Regiment of Foot (Lieutenant-Colonel John Hicks)

1st Battalion 79th Regiment of Foot (Lieutenant-Colonel Neil Douglas)

1st Battalion 95th Regiment of Foot (Lieutenant-Colonel Sir Andrew Barnard)

9th (British) Infantry Brigade

Commanding Officer: Major-General Sir Denis Pack

3rd Battalion 1st Regiment of Foot (Lieutenant-Colonel Colin Campbell)

1st Battalion 42nd Regiment of Foot (Lieutenant-Colonel Sir Robert Macara)

2nd Battalion 44th Regiment of Foot (Lieutenant-Colonel John Hamerton)

1st Battalion 92nd Regiment of Foot (Lieutenant-Colonel John Cameron)

Divisional Artillery

No 2 Company, 3rd Battalion Royal Artillery (Brevet Major Thomas Rogers)

6th (British) Infantry Division
87 officers and 2,582 men

4th (Hanoverian) Infantry Brigade

Commanding Officer: Colonel Carl Best

Verden Landwehr Battalion (Major Christoph von der Decken)

Lüneburg Landwehr Battalion (Lieutenant-Colonel Ludwig Ramdohr)

Osterode Landwehr Battalion (Major Baron Claus von Reden)

Münden Landwehr Battalion (Major Ferdinand von Schmidt)

Brunswick Corps
329 officers and 6,730 men

Commanding Officer: Lieutenant-General Friedrich Wilhelm, Duke of Brunswick

Corps Commandant: Colonel Elias Olfermann

Avantgarde

Avantgarde Battalion (Major Adolph von Rauschenplatt)

Light Infantry Brigade

Commanding Officer: Lieutenant-Colonel Wilhelm Treusch von und zu Buttlar

Leib Battalion (Major Friedrich von Pröstler)

1st Light Battalion (Major Werner von Holstein)

2nd Light Battalion (Major Heinrich von Brandenstein)

3rd Light Battalion (Major Ludwig Ebeling)

Line Infantry Brigade

Commanding Officer: Lieutenant-Colonel Friedrich von Specht

1st Line Battalion (Major Ferdinand Metzner)

2nd Line Battalion (Major Johann von Strombeck)

3rd Line Battalion (Major Gustav von Normann)

Brunswick Cavalry

Hussars Regiment (Major Friedrich von Cramm)

Uhlans Regiment (Major Carl Pott)

Brunswick Artillery

Horse Artillery Battery (Major August Mahn)

Foot Battery (Major Carl Moll)

Nassau-Usingen
53 officers and 2,788 men

Commanding Officer: Major-General Baron August von Kruse

Chief of Staff: Captain Ignaz von Morenhoffen

1st Nassau-Usingen Regiment: Colonel Ernst von Steuben

1st Battalion (Major Wilhelm von Weyhers)

2nd Battalion (Major Adolph von Nauendorf)

3rd Battalion (Major Friedrich von Preen)

BRITISH CAVALRY CORPS
55 OFFICERS AND 760 MEN
3rd (British) Cavalry Brigade

Commanding Officer: Major-General Sir Wilhelm von Dörnberg

23rd Regiment of Light Dragoons (Lieutenant-Colonel John Dawson)

4th (British) Cavalry Brigade

Commanding Officer: Major-General Sir John Ormsby Vandeleur

11th Regiment of Light Dragoons (Lieutenant-Colonel James Sleigh)

Detachment from the Prussian Army

1. Schlesisches Husaren-Regiment (Seconde-Lieutenant Karl von Sellin)

50 all ranks

FRENCH FORCES AT QUATRE BRAS

Commanding Officer: Maréchal Michel Ney, Duc d'Elchingen, Prince de la Moskowa

Aide-de-camp: Colonel Pierre-Agathe Heymès

I CORPS

Commanding Officer: Lieutenant-général Jean-Baptiste Drouet, Comte d'Erlon

Chief of Staff: Maréchal-de-camp Baron Victor-Joseph Delcambre

Commanding Artillery: Maréchal-de-camp Baron Victor-Abel Dessalles

Commanding Engineers: Maréchal-de-camp Baron Marie-Théodore Garbé

1st Infantry Division
181 officers and 4,071 men

Commanding Officer: Maréchal-de-camp Baron Joachim-Jérôme Quiot du Passage

1st Brigade

Commanding Officer: Colonel Chevalier Charles Charlet

54e Régiment d'Infanterie de Ligne (Major Jean-Baptiste Lagneau)

55e Régiment d'Infanterie de Ligne (Colonel Jean-Pierre Monneret)

2nd Brigade

Commanding Officer: Maréchal-de-camp Baron Charles-François Bourgeois

28e Régiment d'Infanterie de Ligne (Colonel Marc-Antoine de Saint-Michel)

105e Régiment d'Infanterie de Ligne (Colonel Jean Genty)

Divisional Artillery

20e Compagnie, 6e Régiment d'Artillerie à Pied (Capitaine Hamelin)

5e Compagnie, 1er Escadron du Train d'Artillerie (Capitaine Paleprat)

Divisional Engineers

1er Compagnie, 2e Bataillon 1er Régiment du Sapeurs (Capitaine Gibou)

2nd Infantry Division
196 officers and 5,191 men

Commanding Officer: Lieutenant-général Baron François-Xavier Donzelot

1st Brigade

Commanding Officer: Maréchal-de-camp Baron Nicolas Schmitz

13e Régiment d'Infanterie Léger (Colonel Pierre Gougeon)

17e Régiment d'Infanterie de Ligne (Colonel Nicolas-Nöel Gueurel)

2nd Brigade

Commanding Officer: Maréchal-de-camp

Baron Pierre Aulard

19e Régiment d'Infanterie de Ligne (Colonel Jean-Aimable Trupel)

51e Régiment d'Infanterie de Ligne (Colonel Jean-Antoine Rignon)

Divisional Artillery

10e Compagnie, 6e Régiment d'Artillerie à Pied (Capitaine Coutin)

9e Compagnie, 1er Escadron du Train d'Artillerie (Capitaine Vaillant)

Divisional Engineers

2e Compagnie, 2e Bataillon 1er Régiment du Sapeurs (Capitaine Fontaine)

II CORPS

Commanding Officer: Lieutenant-général Honoré-Charles, Comte Reille

Chief of Staff: Lieutenant-général Baron Joseph-François Pamphile-Lacroix

Commanding Artillery: Maréchal-de-camp Baron Jean-Baptiste le Pelletier

Commanding Engineers: Maréchal-de-camp Baron Louis-Auguste de Richemont

5th Infantry Division
249 officers and 5,326 men

Commanding Officer: Lieutenant-général Baron Gilbert-Désirée Bachelu

1st Brigade

Commanding Officer: Maréchal-de-camp Baron Pierre-Antoine Husson

2e Régiment d'Infanterie Léger (Colonel Pierre-François Maigrot)

61e Régiment d'Infanterie de Ligne (Colonel Charles Bouge)

2nd Brigade

Commanding Officer: Maréchal-de-camp Baron Toussaint Campi

72e Régiment d'Infanterie de Ligne (Colonel Fréderic-Armand Thibault)

108e Régiment d'Infanterie de Ligne (Colonel Philippe Higonet)

Divisional Artillery

18e Compagnie, 6e Régiment d'Artillerie à Pied (Capitaine Deshaulles)

3e Compagnie, 1er Escadron du Train d'Artillerie (Capitaine Valette)

Divisional Engineers

3e Compagnie, 1er Bataillon 1er Régiment du Sapeurs (Capitaine Vauchout)

6th Infantry Division
239 officers and 6,465 men
Commanding Officer: Lieutenant-général Prince Jérôme Bonaparte
1st Brigade
Commanding Officer: Maréchal-de-camp Baron Pierre-François Bauduin
1er Régiment d'Infanterie Léger (Colonel Amédée-Louis Cubières)
3e Régiment d'Infanterie de Ligne (Colonel Baron Hubert Vautrin)
2nd Brigade
Commanding Officer: Maréchal-de-camp Baron Jean-Louis Soye
1er Régiment d'Infanterie de Ligne (Major Jean-Louis Lebeau)
2e Régiment d'Infanterie de Ligne (Colonel Jean Trippe)
Divisional Artillery
2e Compagnie, 2é Régiment d'Artillerie à Pied (Capitaine Meunier)
1er Compagnie, 1er Escadron du Train d'Artillerie (Capitaine Fivel)
Divisional Engineers
2e Compagnie, 1er Bataillon 1er Régiment de Sapeurs (Capitaine Sabatin)

9th Infantry Division
212 officers and 4,861 men
Commanding Officer: Lieutenant-général Maximilien-Sébastien, Comte Foy
1st Brigade
Commanding Officer: Maréchal-de-camp Baron Jean-Joseph Gauthier
92e Régiment d'Infanterie de Ligne (Colonel Jean-Marie Tissot)
93e Régiment d'Infanterie de Ligne (Chef-de-bataillon Nicolas-François Massot)
2nd Brigade
Commanding Officer: Maréchal-de-camp Baron Jean-Baptiste Jamin
4e Régiment d'Infanterie Léger (Colonel Vincent Peyris)
100e Régiment d'Infanterie de Ligne (Colonel Joseph Braun)
Divisional Artillery
1er Compagnie, 6e Régiment d'Artillerie à Pied (Capitaine Tacon)
2e Compagnie, 1er Escadron du Train d'Artillerie (Capitaine Hubert)

Divisional Engineers
5e Compagnie, 1er Bataillon 1er Régiment de Sapeurs (Capitaine Charve)

2nd Cavalry Division
139 officers and 1,862 men
Commanding Officer: Lieutenant-général Hippolyte-Marie, Comte Piré
1st Brigade
Commanding Officer: Maréchal-de-camp Baron Pierre-François Huber
1er Régiment de Chasseurs à Cheval (Colonel Pierre-Joseph Simonneau)
6e Régiment de Chasseurs à Cheval (Colonel Paul-Eugène de Faudouas)
2nd Brigade
Commanding Officer: Maréchal-de-camp Baron François-Isidore Wathiez
5e Régiment de Chevau-Légers-Lanciers (Colonel Jean-François Jacqueminot)
6e Régiment de Chevau-Légers-Lanciers (Colonel Nicolas-Marie de Galbois)
Divisional Artillery
2e Compagnie, 4e Régiment d'Artillerie à Cheval (Capitaine Gronnier)
2e Compagnie, 5e Escadron du Train d'Artillerie (Capitaine Malherbe)

Reserve Artillery
6 officers and 210 men
7e Compagnie, 2e Régiment d'Artillerie à Pied (Capitaine Valnet)
7e Compagnie, 1er Escadron du Train d'Artillerie (Capitaine Gayat)

Reserve Engineers
4 officers and 85 men
4e Compagnie, 1er Bataillon 1er Régiment du Sapeurs (Capitaine Clausel)

I RESERVE CAVALRY CORPS
36 OFFICERS AND 489 MEN
*1er Régiment de Hussards (Colonel François-Joseph Clary)
*en vedette between Quatre Bras and Nivelles

III RESERVE CAVALRY CORPS
Commanding Officer: Lieutenant-général François-Étienne Kellermann, Comte Valmy

Chief of Staff: Colonel Charles-Antoine de Tancarville

11th Cavalry Division
145 officers and 1,917 men
Commanding Officer: Lieutenant-général Samuel-François, Baron l'Héritier
1st Brigade
Commanding Officer: Maréchal-de-camp Baron Cyrille-Simon Picquet
2e Régiment de Dragons (Colonel François-Joseph Planzeaux)
7e Régiment de Dragons (Charles-Philippe Léopold)
2nd Brigade
Commanding Officer: Maréchal-de-camp Baron Marie-Adrien Guiton
8e Régiment de Cuirassiers (Colonel Antoine-Laurent Garavaque)
11e Régiment de Cuirassiers (Colonel Eleonore-Ambroise Courtier)
Divisional Artillery
3e Compagnie, 2e Régiment d'Artillerie à Cheval (Capitaine Marcillac)
3e Compagnie, 2e Escadron du Train d'Artillerie (Lieutenant Dupont)

Light Cavalry Division of the Garde Impériale
95 officers and 1,771 men
Commanding Officer: Lieutenant-Général Charles, Comte Lefèbvre-Desnouettes
1st Brigade
Régiment de Chasseurs à Cheval de la Garde Impériale (Lieutenant-général Baron François-Antoine Lallemand)
2nd Brigade
Régiment de Chevau-Légers-Lanciers de la Garde Impériale (Lieutenant-général Baron Édouard de Colbert-Chabanais)
**One squadron detached at Fleurus as 'Duty Squadron' to Napoleon
Divisional Artillery
1er Compagnie de Régiment d'Artillerie à Cheval de la Garde (Capitaine Huet)
2e Compagnie de Régiment d'Artillerie à Cheval de la Garde (Capitaine Nasse)

OPPOSING PLANS

Having concentrated their armies in the Low Countries, the Duke of Wellington and Feldmarschall Blücher were patiently awaiting the arrival of their respective coalition partners on the eastern border of France. This was expected to be achieved in early July, whereupon the entire force would invade in such overwhelming numbers that they believed victory would be inevitable. Unbeknown to the various members of the coalition, the duke had made arrangements for King Louis XVIII, who was at Ghent, to follow the Allied Army and, in accordance with the wishes of the British Parliament, to use his influence to re-establish him on the throne of France once the fighting had been concluded.

Prior to the outbreak of hostilities Wellington and Blücher had agreed to concentrate their respective armies at Nivelles and Sombreffe in the event of a French attack. The two commanders reasoned that their combined force would be sufficient to repel any such eventuality. But the wide deployment of the Allied Army, which was dictated by the necessity to safeguard the ports of Antwerp and Ostend, aligned with the duke's reluctance to act until he was absolutely sure of the French line of advance, meant they were susceptible to a strategy Napoleon had employed with great success in a number of his previous campaigns, namely that of the central position.

By advancing rapidly and interposing the French Army between the two opposing forces, Napoleon planned to separate and to defeat each in detail, or to drive them back along their lines of communication. The contemporary evidence suggests that Napoleon expected the coalition armies to retire, rather than engage in battle, and expose Brussels to his advance without there being a serious engagement. This is one of the crucial elements to understanding the early stages of the campaign, and the engagement at Quatre Bras in particular, because neither of the combatants was expecting an action to take place at the crossroads.

In order to execute his plans Napoleon divided the French Army into two wings and a reserve. The left column was composed of I and II Corps, which were initially positioned around Solre-sur-Sambre and Leers et Fosteau; the centre consisted of III and VI Corps, the cavalry and the artillery reserves, and the Garde Impériale, all of whom were stationed near Beaumont; while IV Corps at Philippeville formed the right column. Employment of this strategy and formation resulted in simultaneous actions being fought at Quatre Bras and Ligny on 16 June, the former being a subsidiary of the latter, in almost exactly the same manner that it led to battles being fought two days later at Mont St Jean and Wavre.

THE CAMPAIGN OPENS

In the cold grey light before dawn the French II Corps, under the command of Comte Reille, advanced from its position at Leers et Fosteau and crossed the frontier. The column followed the road along the right bank of the Sambre River, and at 3:30pm the vanguard came into contact with the Prussian outposts in front of Thuin. Despite the difficult terrain the French drove the enemy back to the village of Montigny-le-Tilleul, where the fighting intensified. The Prussians retired slowly towards the bridge at Marchienne-au-Pont, but they were overwhelmed by a charge from the 1er Régiment de Chasseurs à Cheval, and more than 100 men were cut down. The French infantry moved rapidly against the defenders. After a violent exchange of fire the 2e Régiment Léger from Baron Pierre-Antoine Husson's Brigade attacked with the bayonet. The French crossed the bridge with the utmost haste and the Prussians withdrew in the face of the formidable onslaught. With the bridge and both banks along the Sambre having been secured, the French vanguard continued its march towards Brussels.

While the left wing of the French Army was making steady progress towards Charleroi, the right wing at Philippeville, commanded by Comte Gérard, was delayed by an act of betrayal. The orders issued the previous evening had specified that the right column was to advance more slowly than the left and the centre, and this circumstance afforded Louis de Ghaisnes, Comte Bourmont, an ardent royalist, the opportunity to defect. Having led the 14th Division across the border at Florennes, Comte Bourmont and five staff officers who shared his sympathies rode forward under the pretext of making a reconnaissance of the area. The group dismissed their escort with a letter for the corps commander, then donned white Bourbon cockades and continued into the enemy lines. They were removed to the cantonments at Fosses-la-Ville, where Comte Bourmont furnished the Prussians with all of the information at his disposal.

News of the defection was sent to Napoleon at Jamignon, and subsequently he ordered Comte Gérard to direct his troops to the bridge at Châtelet, 4 miles to the east of Charleroi, which they reached late in the day. The emperor had also been informed of the situation in the centre. The corps commanded by Comtes Vandamme and Lobau, with the Garde Impériale and the reserve cavalry,

Édouard (Pierre-David) de Colbert-Chabanais was a distinctive cavalryman with an exemplary service record. During the campaign he resumed his position at the head of the Chevau-Légers Lanciers of the Garde Impériale. (Private Collection, France. Photo © Ronald Pawly)

were the last to be put in motion, for although they were the nearest to imperial headquarters, the orders sent to Comte Vandamme had failed to be executed in the manner the emperor had prescribed, due in part to the difficult terrain. This had resulted in a lengthy delay. Order was eventually restored, and the column moved forward in the direction of Jamioulx. However, I Reserve Cavalry Corps, which formed part of the cavalry under Maréchal Grouchy, had advanced and engaged the Prussian outposts at Ham-sur-Heure, forcing a passage to the dyke connecting Marcinelles with Charleroi. The intervening bridge across the Sambre had been barricaded and was defended by Prussian skirmishers, who lined the hedge and ditches along the slope of the embankment. The French horsemen attempted to carry the bridge, but were driven back, and so Napoleon ordered the *marins* and the *sapeurs* of the Garde Impériale to support the light cavalry. Towards 11:00am the French renewed the attack, and confronted by superior numbers the Prussian rearguard abandoned the town and retired in the direction of Gilly and Gosselies.

Having secured the bridges across the Sambre and captured Charleroi, the French continued their advance. Maréchal Grouchy and Comte Vandamme were ordered to take the Sombreffe road to Fleurus, while the 1er Régiment de Hussards was pushed forward on the road towards Brussels. The latter was supplemented by the light cavalry of the Garde Impériale, under the command of Charles, Comte Lefèbvre-Desnouettes, and at 3:00pm by Comte Reille and II Corps, which was ordered to attack the Prussians at Gosselies. Shortly thereafter, the French received a reinforcement in the form of Maréchal Michel Ney. Accompanied by his aide-de-camp, Colonel Pierre-Agathe Heymès, Ney had followed the army and joined the emperor on the road north of Charleroi. Napoleon was cordial, and immediately gave Ney the command of the left column, with the promise that it would be enhanced in the morning by the two divisions of heavy cavalry under Comte Valmy. He explained that the vanguard was advancing on Gosselies, and instructed the marshal to seize the town and to pursue the enemy. Accordingly, Ney rode forward to animate his men.

The Lanciers Rouges or 2e Régiment de Chevau-Légers of the Garde Impériale, were an elite light cavalry regiment renowned for their loyalty to the emperor and prowess on the battlefield. Print by Martinet. (Bibliothèque Nationale de France, Paris)

Comte Reille was forced to deploy a considerable number of troops from II Corps before the Prussians were dislodged from Gosselies, but believing that he had attained his objective for the day, he established his headquarters and sent a report to Maréchal Soult. However, Ney now arrived and ordered Comte Lefèbvre-Desnouettes to continue with the light cavalry towards Frasnes, and Baron Bachelu to support the movement by occupying Mellet with the 5th Division.

When the division arrived upon the heights close to the village of Frasnes, the vanguard from the 2e Régiment Léger encountered a battalion of Nassau infantry and a battery of horse artillery. The enemy resisted, and only the intervention of French cavalry forced them to retire. The Allied troops retired in perfect order, despite being menaced on all sides, as far as the crossroads at Quatre Bras, at which point the French cavalry were forced to desist. The Lanciers Rouges

Charles, Comte Lefèbvre-Desnouettes, was an outstanding horseman and one of the emperor's most trusted subordinates. He commanded the division of light cavalry of the Garde Impériale in the Low Countries. Painting by Sébastien Weygandt (Musée de l'Armée, Paris / René Chartrand)

of the Garde Impériale and the 1er Régiment de Hussards from I Reserve Cavalry Corps, which had become intermixed during the advance, retired to Frasnes.

As the troops from II Corps came up, they moved into bivouacs for the night. The 5th Division was positioned in front of Mellet. The cavalry division under the command of Lieutenant-général Piré was immediately behind the small village. The divisions commanded by Comte Foy and Jérôme Bonaparte occupied Gosselies, while that of Baron Girard was at Wangenies.

Ney established his headquarters at the Maison Dumont in Gosselies and requested reports from the division commanders, which he duly received. He had been placed in a most difficult position, without staff or prior knowledge of the emperor's overall plan. It was imperative therefore to learn as much as possible during the night while the army was resting. The report Ney received from Comte Lefèbvre-Desnouettes confirmed that Lieutenant-général Colbert had advanced with the Lanciers Rouges of the Garde Impériale to within musket range of Quatre Bras, but as the ground had been difficult and the troops defending the crossroads had maintained a vigorous fire, it had been impossible to carry the position. Darkness had enveloped the field, and so the cavalry retired and bivouacked in rear of Frasnes with a line of outposts covering the nearby wood. Armed with this information Maréchal Ney sent word to Napoleon, who was at Charleroi.

THE NETHERLANDS OFFICERS TAKE THE INITIATIVE

The troops with whom the French had been engaged at Quatre Bras were those of the 2nd Nassau-Usingen Brigade, commanded by Prince Bernhard von Sachsen-Weimar. Colonel Friedrich von Goedecke had initially commanded the brigade, but on 14 June, whilst on the parade ground, he received a severe kick on the shin from the horse belonging to the adjutant of the 2nd Nassau-Usingen Regiment, Lieutenant Friedrich von Steprodt. The injury was such that Colonel von Goedecke felt unable to maintain the command, and so on the morning of the 15 June orders were delivered to Prince Bernhard which assigned the command of the 2nd Brigade to him.

The brigade had been quartered that morning along the road from Frasnes to Genappe, when heavy cannon fire was heard from the direction of Charleroi. This was initially believed to be the Prussian artillery exercising, but as the fire became more distinct in the afternoon Major Philipp von Normann, who was billeted in Frasnes with the 2nd Battalion, 2nd Nassau-Usingen, decided to take precautions. He placed an observation post south of the village on the road to Charleroi, and deployed the remaining troops under his command to the north of the village on the road to Quatre Bras. The battery of horse artillery commanded by Captain Adriaan Bijleveld was positioned on both sides of the high road, while the infantry were drawn in line to the left and right of the guns. Major Normann sent a report to the regimental commander at Houtain-le-Val, Major Johann Sattler, who in turn forwarded the details to the divisional commander, Lieutenant-General Baron Perponcher-Sedlnitsky, whose headquarters were located in Nivelles.

At 6:00pm, when the Lanciers Rouges of the Garde Impériale attacked the outpost at Frasnes, the 1st Flank Company under Captain Johann Müller and 80 volunteers commanded by Lieutenant Wilhelm Höelschen were sent forward. Although a salvo drove the French cavalry back, almost immediately thereafter they threatened the Allied troops on both flanks. Fearing that the battalion would be enveloped, Major Normann ordered the men to withdraw under the cover of steady artillery fire to the farm of Gémioncourt, which was situated halfway between Frasnes and the crossroads at Quatre Bras. This was accomplished in good order and the French cavalry retired.

Prince Bernhard was at Genappe when he received confirmation that the French were advancing from Charleroi. Realizing the urgency of the situation, he ordered the 2nd Brigade to concentrate at Quatre Bras. When Prince Bernhard reached the crossroads with both battalions of the Orange-Nassau Regiment later that evening, he found the 1st and 3rd battalions of the 2nd Nassau-Usingen already assembled and under arms. The troops formed square, as enemy cavalry was seen in the distance, and Prince Bernhard received a full report from Major von Normann. With full knowledge of the importance of the position at Quatre Bras, he placed the 1st Battalion in column on the high road to Houtain-le-Val and detached two companies to line the right edge of the wood. At the same time two companies from the 3rd Battalion, the Grenadier Company of that battalion, as well as two companies from the 2nd Battalion, 28th Orange-Nassau, were sent to reinforce the position the 2nd Nassau-Usingen Battalion had taken in front of the crossroads; the company of Volunteer Jägers was formed into four platoons and detached to cover the wood, while two artillery pieces were placed on the high road to Namur and a 6-pdr deployed in a position close to the main road to Charleroi. The remainder of the troops were held in reserve behind the crossroads. Prince Bernhard then sent a messenger to Baron Perponcher-Sedlnitsky, informing him of the measures he had taken to defend the position and of the inadequacy of the force at his disposal.

Upon receipt of the letter from Prince Bernhard, Baron Perponcher-Sedlnitsky ordered the 1st Brigade of the 2nd Netherlands Division to concentrate at Nivelles and sent one of his adjutants, Baron Friedrich von Gagern, to Quatre Bras with instructions to hold the position for as long as possible, but if attacked by a superior enemy force to retire in the direction of Mont St Jean. Baron von Gagern then rode to the general headquarters in Braine-le-Comte to obtain orders from the Hereditary Prince of Orange-Nassau, and his chief of staff, Baron Jean-Victor de Constant-Rebècque.

The officers and men of the 4th Dutch Light Dragoons formed part of the brigade commanded by Baron Charles de Ghigny, and on the morning of 15 June were in cantonments on the high road between Ville sur Haine and Nivelles. Painting by Jan Hoynck van Papendrecht. (Nationaal Militair Museum (NMM) Soesterberg)

Combat at Frasnes, 6:00pm, 15 June 1815

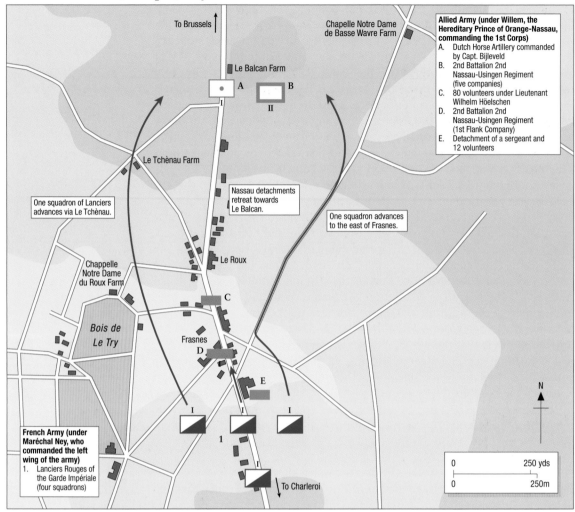

To Brussels

Chapelle Notre Dame
de Basse Wavre Farm

Le Balcan Farm

A   B

II

Le Tchènau Farm

One squadron of Lanciers
advances via Le Tchènau.

Nassau detachments
retreat towards
Le Balcan.

One squadron advances
to the east of Frasnes.

Le Roux

Chappelle
Notre Dame
du Roux Farm

C

Bois de
Le Try

Frasnes

D

E

N

Allied Army (under Willem, the Hereditary Prince of Orange-Nassau, commanding the 1st Corps)
A. Dutch Horse Artillery commanded by Capt. Bijleveld
B. 2nd Battalion 2nd Nassau-Usingen Regiment (five companies)
C. 80 volunteers under Lieutenant Wilhelm Höelschen
D. 2nd Battalion 2nd Nassau-Usingen Regiment (1st Flank Company)
E. Detachment of a sergeant and 12 volunteers

French Army (under Maréchal Ney, who commanded the left wing of the army)
1. Lanciers Rouges of the Garde Impériale (four squadrons)

1

To Charleroi

0   250 yds
0   250m

The prince had risen at first light and ridden south to the border to undertake a routine inspection of the light cavalry outposts, where the troops had been under arms since 5:00am. Having received no adverse news of the French Army, and seeing that everything was perfectly quiet, he returned to Braine-le-Comte and after breakfasting set off at 9:30am for Brussels, where he was to dine with the Duke of Wellington at 3:00pm, before attending a ball being given that evening by Charlotte, Duchess of Richmond. However, towards midday Baron Constant-Rebècque received a communication from Major-General Johann Behr at Mons that the Prussians had been attacked that morning in front of Thuin and that the Prussian detachment occupying Binche had retreated to Gosselies. He immediately forwarded this information to the Hereditary Prince at Brussels, and sent an order to Baron Perponcher-Sedlnitsky to assemble his 1st Brigade on the high road close to Nivelles and his 2nd Brigade at Quatre Bras. Orders were also sent to generals Chassé and Collaert to assemble their divisions, the first at Faijt and the second behind Haine St Pierre.

Vague reports of the French offensive continued to arrive at Braine-le-Comte during the course of the day, where Baron Constant-Rebècque and Lieutenant-Colonel Sir George Berkeley collated the information and forwarded the relevant intelligence to Brussels. At 9:00pm they received a letter from the Prince, in which he stated that it was his intention to remain in the capital until the early hours, and that unless they believed otherwise, there was no reason to keep the troops under arms all night.

At 10:00pm Baron von Gagern arrived and reported that the French had advanced as far as the crossroads at Quatre Bras, where the token force commanded by Bernhard von Sachsen-Weimar had held them. Shortly thereafter, a letter with orders from the Duke of Wellington in Brussels was delivered by Captain the Hon Francis Russell, one of the prince's aides-de-camp. These stated that the 2nd and 3rd Netherlands divisions were to collect at Nivelles, and that the cavalry was to collect on the height behind Haine St Pierre. Execution of these orders would have resulted in the Nassau troops abandoning the crossroads at Quatre Bras. The enormity of the situation was clear to Baron Constant-Rebècque: no one within the duke's headquarters knew of the French attack upon Quatre Bras. He immediately dispatched another of the prince's aides-de-camp, Lieutenant Henry Webster, to Brussels with a letter informing His Royal Highness of the true state of affairs. Thereafter, Count Otto van Limburg Stirum, one of the adjoints on the staff of the 1st Corps, was sent to Baron Perponcher-Sedlnitsky with instructions to defend Quatre Bras resolutely, and that the 1st Brigade was to reinforce the troops already at the crossroads.

John Cameron of Fassifern commanded the 92nd (Gordon Highland) Regiment of Foot at the beginning of the campaign in the Low Countries. Painting by Charles Turner. (Clan Cameron Museum)

APATHY IN THE CAPITAL TOWARDS A FRENCH ATTACK

The Hereditary Prince of Orange-Nassau had arrived in Brussels shortly after 3:00pm and informed the Duke of Wellington of the French attack upon the Prussian outpost at Thuin while they were at dinner. This information was corroborated by the Prussian officer attached to the British headquarters, Generalmajor Karl, Freiherr von Müffling. He confirmed that the Prussians were concentrating at Sombreffe, and consequently Feldmarschall Blücher wished to know the concentration point of the Allied Army. The duke explained that until he had received a decisive report of the French movements from his outpost at Mons he was unable to specify the rendezvous point, but at 6:00pm he issued orders for the troops to assemble at their respective headquarters.

The situation within the Allied Army was complicated by the fact that a large number of senior officers had already left their respective cantonments for Brussels to attend the ball being given later that evening by the Duchess of Richmond. Indeed, it was late into the night before

Charlotte, Duchess of Richmond, was a member of the Gordon family and therefore shared a strong bond with the officers and men of the 92nd Regiment. A small party performed sword dancing and reels at her function, much to the delight of the guests. Print by Genty. (Bibliothèque Nationale de France, Paris)

the various divisions received the order to hold themselves in readiness to move at a moment's notice, by which time guests had begun to arrive at the function in the rue de la Blanchisserie. The guests were a mixture of civil and military dignitaries and those highly placed within British or Belgian society. Rumours had been circulating in the capital during the course of the day that the French had forced the Prussian line and taken the village of Binche. The civilians in attendance naturally questioned the military personnel on the validity of the story, but none were in a position to confirm the truth. Everyone awaited the arrival of the Duke of Wellington.

The duke had been making his preparations, when shortly before midnight he received confirmation from the outpost at Mons that the entire French force had marched towards Charleroi. He therefore issued supplementary orders to the Allied Army, specifying the various concentration points. Freiherr von Müffling was informed that the troops had been directed upon Nivelles and Quatre Bras, and that despite the imminent movement he planned to attend the ball being given by the Duchess of Richmond.

In actual fact the information the duke had given to Freiherr von Müffling was incorrect, as none of the troops had actually been ordered to Quatre Bras. The orders specified that the troops in Brussels, being the 5th and 6th Divisions, the Duke of Brunswick's contingent and the Nassau, were to march when assembled from Brussels along the Namur road to the point where the road to Nivelles separates. These troops were to be followed by Major-General Dörnberg's brigade and the Cumberland Hussars. The 3rd Division was ordered to continue its movement from Braine-le-Comte upon Nivelles, while the 1st Division was to move from Enghien to Braine-le-Comte. The 2nd and 4th divisions were ordered to move from Ath, Grammont and Audenarde towards Enghien. Finally, the cavalry was ordered to move from Ninove to Enghien. These movements were to be undertaken with the

The Duchess of Richmond's ball was one of many lavish functions held in Brussels during June 1815. As a considerable number of senior Allied officers were present the Duke of Wellington had the opportunity to impart specific verbal orders. Painting by Robert Hillingford. (Goodwood House, Surrey)

minimum delay. However, it would be several hours before many units received these new directives, due to the difficulty the messengers encountered in finding their way on the country roads during the hours of darkness.

When the Duke of Wellington eventually arrived at the ball Lady Georgiana Lennox accosted him. She asked if the rumours of a French attack upon the Prussians were true, and was surprised when the duke confirmed they were, and that the Allied Army would be set in motion at first light the following morning. The news swept rapidly through the building and several officers immediately bade their hostess farewell and departed. However, the Duke of Wellington continued to project an air of gaiety and cheerfulness, as if oblivious to the impending danger.

Lavish functions were a regular feature of the social calendar in Brussels, and because of this the Duchess of Richmond had arranged for the guests to be treated to a display of Highland sword dancing and reels by members of the 92nd Regiment of Foot, the Gordon Highlanders. The spectacle was born out of the relationship she enjoyed with the regiment, and the many Belgian civilians in attendance were struck by the skill of the performance, much to the satisfaction of the regiment's colonel, John Cameron, who was among the guests. At the conclusion of the demonstration the guests were invited to ascend the stairs as supper was ready to be served, and it was now that the details of the French attack were revealed to the Duke of Wellington and his subordinates.

Lieutenant Henry Webster had arrived in the capital shortly after midnight with the letter from Baron Constant-Rebècque. Having been redirected from His Royal Highness's residence to the address in the rue de la Blanchisserie, he had made his way through the mass of carriages and persuaded the porter to allow him to pass. Webster hastened inside and handed the note to the Hereditary Prince, who immediately passed it to the duke and signalled for his aide-de-camp to remain downstairs. Wellington waited until he was seated before reading the message, which confirmed the French had reached Quatre Bras. The shocking news was not conveyed to the other guests. The duke went back downstairs and instructed Webster to prepare the prince's horses and carriage so that he could return to Braine-le-Comte immediately. Returning upstairs, he whispered instructions to the Hereditary Prince and Duke of Brunswick, both of whom made their excuses and departed before supper was served. Word was passed discreetly to the various Allied officers in attendance, and within minutes of the guests adjourning to the ballroom downstairs, they had departed. But Wellington and his Military Secretary, Lord Fitzroy Somerset, remained until 3:00am, studying a map with the Duke of Richmond. This confirmed that the action taken by the Netherlands officers had secured the direct line of communication with the Prussians at Sombreffe. The situation could therefore be redeemed.

A romantic portrayal of the Duke of Wellington and the Allied Army marching on the high road to Quatre Bras on 16 June. The artist has also painted an officer of the Foot Guards wearing the silk stockings he supposedly wore the previous evening at the ball given by the Duchess of Richmond. Painting by Robert Hillingford. (Private collection)

View of the crossroads at Quatre Bras in the distance, with cavalry passing through the village of Thyle and moving along the road from Namur. Coloured engraving by James Rouse. (The Stapleton Collection / Bridgeman Images)

Bernhard von Sachsen-Weimer was only 23 years of age at the time the command of the 2nd Brigade devolved upon him. However, he was an experienced officer, having served in both the Prussian and Saxon armies prior to the campaign. Painting by Rudolph Suhrlandt. (Klassik Stiftung Museum, Weimar)

MOVEMENTS ON THE MORNING OF 16 JUNE

At 3:30am the Hereditary Prince of Orange-Nassau returned to his headquarters in Braine-le-Comte and was immediately met by Baron Constant-Rebècque. The prince approved of the measures his chief of staff had taken, particularly the reinforcement of Quatre Bras. However, he still believed that the enemy would direct his forces against Nivelles. He therefore ordered Baron Constant-Rebècque to ride to Quatre Bras ahead of him and to inform the troops at Nivelles to be ready to march.

Prince Bernhard von Sachsen-Weimar was mounted on his horse in front of the inn at Quatre Bras together with the officer commanding the 2nd Netherlands Division, Baron Perponcher-Sedlnitsky, when Baron Constant-Rebècque arrived shortly before 5:30am. It was a bright, sunny morning and the day was expected to be very hot, so Baron Perponcher-Sedlnitsky had left Nivelles at first light with the 27th Jägers and the 8th Militia Battalion in order to reinforce the post and to assume the command. While on the high road they had encountered a detachment of 50 Prussian cavalrymen from the 1. Schlesisches Husaren-Regiment led by Seconde-Lieutenant Karl von Sellin. The cavalry had been separated from its brigade during the fighting on the 15th, and having no cavalry at his disposal Baron Perponcher-Sedlnitsky suggested that they accompany him to the crossroads.

The hamlet of Quatre Bras marked the junction of the roads from Brussels to Charleroi and Namur to Nivelles, and consisted of an inn, a farmhouse and a number of smaller dwellings. To the west of the crossroads was a wood called the Bois de Bossu, which stretched south as far as the farms of Grand and Petit Pierrepont, and to the east was the village of Piraumont. The intervening valley was a succession of cornfields traversed by a wide stream and a pond, and adjacent to the high road, half way to Frasnes, stood the farm of Gémioncourt. These quiet pastures now assumed greater significance than the Duke of Wellington had originally envisaged, for when he had formulated his plans for the defence of the realm against a French attack, he had considered Nivelles as the primary point upon which the Allied Army would pivot. This was reflected in the orders the duke had issued during the course of the previous evening. However, the threat to Quatre Bras endangered his ability to communicate directly with the Prussian Army.

Shortly after 6:00am the Hereditary Prince arrived and together with his chief of staff he rode along the outposts formed by the troops of the Nassau-Usingen Regiment. The French *tirailleurs* were positioned only a short distance away, and they opened fire from the cover of the wheat, which was very high. On the height in front of Frasnes, by the Bois de l'Hutte, were a considerable number of *chasseurs à cheval* and *lanciers*, and now the small detachment of Prussian cavalrymen displayed the utmost spirit. They skirmished with the enemy and made several charges against the *lanciers*, so as to make the French believe that the Allied force at the crossroads was greater in size than it actually was. The prince ordered the 2nd Battalion 2nd Nassau-Usingen to advance. This movement was supported by the 27th Jägers, and the Allied troops forced the enemy cavalry patrols to withdraw and regained almost all of the ground which had been lost the previous day. A line of skirmishers was able to move further forward and to conceal itself amidst the high corn, while the artillery was positioned so as to cover the roads from Charleroi and Namur.

Bernhard von Sachsen-Weimar (second right) is shown discussing the situation at Quatre Bras with the senior officers from the 2nd Brigade. Painting by Jan Hoynck van Papendrecht. (Nationaal Militair Museum (NMM) Soesterberg)

At this time Major Friedrich von Brünneck, adjutant to Feldmarschall Blücher, arrived at Quatre Bras with orders to ascertain the situation and strength of the Allied force. His Royal Highness appraised the Prussian staff officer with the positions and proposed movements of the divisions within the Allied Army, and this information was immediately communicated to the Prussian high command. Having learned the whereabouts of his brigade from Major von Brünneck, Seconde-Lieutenant von Sellin requested permission to rejoin it, and this being granted the Prussian cavalrymen departed for the Sombreffe.

IMPORTANT DECISIONS FOR THE THREE COMMANDERS

Brussels was a sea of motion as the army reserve assembled in the park and spent the night preparing for the impending departure. The order to move was finally delivered at 4:00am and, as the shrill of the pipes and the beat of the drums rent the morning air, the troops marched out of the city by the gates of the Porte de Namur. The highland troops from Sir Thomas Picton's division marched to the tune of 'Highland Laddie'. The officers and men appeared to be in high spirits, and nothing could be more martial or more imposing than their appearance. Other British regiments followed, then the Nassau, and at 8:00am the Duke of Wellington and his staff rode out of the capital.

The duke and his party stopped at the farm of Mont St Jean, on the edge of the Forêt de Soignes, where he conversed with Sir Thomas Picton, whose division had halted in the shade of the trees to cook. Wellington was wearing a plain blue frockcoat, white breeches, a white neck-cloth and a small bicorne hat, as was his custom. Thereafter, the Allied commander and his entourage continued their journey, and they arrived at Quatre Bras shortly after 10:00am. Having reconnoitred the field and complimented the Hereditary Prince of Orange-Nassau on the deployment of the troops, the duke was introduced to Major von Brünneck by Freiherr von Müffling. A polite discussion ensued. Wellington wrote a short letter to Feldmarschall Blücher, outlining the situation with the Allied Army; but finding everything surprisingly quiet, at 12:30pm he resolved to ride to the Prussian headquarters at the windmill of Bussy at Brye, to verbally agree the measures for a decisive battle.

Napoleon spent the night at Charleroi, where at daybreak he instructed Maréchal Soult, the major-général, to inform Maréchal Ney, who commanded the left wing of the French Army, that the cavalry under Comte Valmy was being placed at his disposal, and also to request an update on the position of I Corps, which had bivouacked the night before at Marchienne-au-Pont. Napoleon remained in his headquarters collating the intelligence and deliberating the subsequent movements of the French Army, when towards 6:00pm a report arrived from Maréchal Grouchy, who was with the right wing of the army, stating that the Prussians were deploying at Fleurus. Consequently, the emperor determined the dispositions of the various French corps, and directed Maréchal Soult to issue corresponding orders, while he dictated a letter to Maréchal Ney.

He informed his estranged commander that he would receive orders relating to the movements of the left wing from Maréchal Soult in due course, but his aide-de-camp Charles, Comte de Flahaut, had been charged with the delivery of the letter he had dictated as it was of great importance. Napoleon explained

During the campaign in 1815 Charles, Comte de Flahaut de la Billarderie, was one of Napoleon's personal aides-de-camp. Having delivered the emperor's message to Maréchal Ney, he remained at Quatre Bras for the remainder of the day. Painting by François Gèrard. (The Trustees of the Bowood Collection)

that Maréchal Grouchy would be sent with III and IV Corps towards Sombreffe, and he would follow with the Garde Impériale and attack any enemy troops that they encountered, before reconnoitring in the direction of Gembloux. There, according to what had transpired, he would decide upon the subsequent movements, but it was his intention that Ney should move towards Brussels, arriving in the capital the following morning. To achieve this Napoleon proposed to support the left wing with the Garde Impériale, which would be stationed at Fleurus or Sombreffe. If there were no obstacles, Ney was to deploy his troops so that one division was placed 2 miles in front of Quatre Bras, with a total of six divisions around the crossroads. One division was to be at Marbais, in order to move closer to the Sombreffe, should the emperor need support. The cavalry corps under the command of Comte Valmy comprising 3,000 *cuirassiers*, was to be posted at the intersection of the old Roman road and the high road to Brussels. Ney was also to return the cavalry of the Garde Impériale commanded by Comte Lefèbvre-Desnouettes.

The letter continued by explaining the plan he had devised to exploit the advantage they had gained over their opponents. As a general principle Napoleon would divide the army into two wings and a reserve. The left wing which Ney commanded would be composed of the four divisions of I Corps, the four divisions of II Corps and the two divisions commanded by Comte Valmy. This would total between 40,000 and 50,000 men. Maréchal Grouchy would have a force of similar strength with the right wing. The Garde Impériale would form the reserve and he, the emperor, would join with either wing, depending on the circumstances.

Finally, Napoleon emphasized the importance of taking Brussels, which would isolate the British Army from Mons, Ostend and so on. He therefore wished to have a complete understanding of the dispositions so that upon receipt of the first order, Ney would be able to move with the eight divisions under his command without delay towards Brussels. Maréchal Grouchy was sent a similar letter with instructions for the right wing, and thereafter, the emperor moved with the imperial headquarters to Fleurus.

The officers and men of the 27th Dutch Jägers Battalion skirmished with the French Tirailleurs during the morning of 16 June, but were eventually overwhelmed by sheer weight of numbers. Painting by Gerry Embleton. (Private collection)

Towards 11:00am Comte de Flahaut reached Frasnes with the letter for Maréchal Ney. He had passed through Gosselies and informed Comte Reille of the order, so as to hasten the concentration of II Corps, and also to ensure that Comte d'Erlon was acquainted with the proposed movement. Upon receipt of the message Ney sent word to the respective officers to march immediately with their corps and to occupy the crossroads at Quatre Bras, while the cavalry of the Garde Impériale were directed to remain in their position at Frasnes until relieved by the divisions under Comte Valmy. The 1er Régiment de Hussards, which had remained with the left wing, were detached between Quatre Bras and Nivelles to cover the left flank prior to the commencement of hostilities. However, some considerable time was required before the orders could be executed by the various divisions. The 9th Division left Gosselies towards midday, followed by the two divisions of heavy cavalry and the 6th Division commanded by Jérôme Bonaparte, and it was 1:00pm before the first of these troops reached Frasnes. Without waiting for the entire force at his disposal to be united, Maréchal Ney ordered Comte Piré and Baron Bachelu to deploy their divisions between the high road and the Bois de l'Hutte, and Comte Foy to form his troops on their left, in readiness to advance.

THE STRUGGLE FOR THE CROSSROADS COMMENCES

The Hereditary Prince of Orange-Nassau had deployed the Allied troops at Quatre Bras across a wide frontage, so as to create the impression of greater strength. The artillery was positioned on the roads from Charleroi and Namur and the area south of the Bois de Bossu. The guns on the high road to Charleroi were covered by two companies from the 27th Jägers Battalion. The rest of the battalion were deployed at Gémioncourt or acted as skirmishers in the cornfields in front of the village of Piraumont. The ground in the centre, north of Gémioncourt, was defended by troops from the 5th Dutch Militia. The Nassau volunteer Jägers and 8th Militia Battalion occupied the extreme right wing, while the remainder of the Allied troops at Quatre Bras were held at the crossroads or positioned in the Bois de Bossu.

Shortly before 2:00pm the 1st battalions of the Nassau-Usingen and Orange-Nassau Regiments were ordered to advance along the high road towards Charleroi and to take positions in the hollow on the right, next to the wood. They had hardly deployed when the enemy advanced to attack Quatre Bras, shelling the wood on their left with cannon and howitzer. Screened by the artillery, and flanked by the *chasseurs à cheval* and the *chevau-leger-lanciers* from Comte Piré's 2nd Cavalry Division, the French advanced in two columns to the east of the high road. The sheer weight of numbers drove the Allied skirmishers back and a cloud of *tirailleurs* moved rapidly against the troops defending Grand and Petit Pierrepont and the Bois de Bossu. While the 1st Brigade of Comte Foy's Division remained on the plateau close to the farm of Lairalle, the 2nd Brigade, commanded by Baron Jean-Baptiste Jamin, marched across the valley towards Gémioncourt. On the right flank the head of the 5th Division, led by Baron Bachelu, engaged the Allies in and around the farm of Piraumont and threw them back.

Lieutenant-Colonel Jan Westenberg depicted leading the 5th Dutch Militia during the fighting at Gémioncourt. The two flank companies were involved in the engagement and sustained heavy losses, while the remainder of the battalion was positioned to the north of the farm. Painting by Piet de Jong. (Nationaal Militair Museum (NMM) Soesterberg)

The *chasseurs* and *lanciers* charged the skirmishers from the 27th Jägers Battalion in the open ground before they had re-formed, and entirely broke them. The battalion lost a great many men killed and wounded, including Lieutenant-Colonel Willem van Grunebosch, and others were taken prisoner. The French infantry advanced rapidly and took possession of Piraumont and the majority of the ground immediately in front of the Allied position. They were now able to direct their efforts towards the centre.

Baron Perponcher-Sedlnitsky had witnessed these events, and realizing that the French had gained a significant advantage, he ordered the 7th Line Battalion to support their comrades in the centre. The battalion advanced into the open ground between the Bois de Bossu and the high road to Charleroi and extended in line. At this time the 5th Militia Battalion advanced in column and deployed on the right of Gémioncourt under heavy canister and musket fire. The farm buildings had been occupied by two companies from the 27th Jägers, and so the two flanker companies from the 5th Militia were hurriedly pushed forward and deployed in front of the complex. But here they suffered from the close-range enemy fire, as the French *tirailleurs* used the high corn as cover, and their numbers were severely depleted.

The French cavalry had re-formed in the hollow ground to the south of Gémioncourt, and they now launched four consecutive charges against the militiamen. Each was repelled, but the incessant enemy artillery and small-arms fire eventually forced the 5th Militia Battalion to retire some distance beyond

The Prince of Orange-Nassau gallantly leads the officers and men of the 5th Dutch Militia back into the fray at Gémioncourt. Painting by Jan Hoynck van Papendrecht. (Nationaal Militair Museum (NMM) Soesterberg)

Another rendition of the moment the Prince of Orange-Nassau led the troops of the 5th Dutch Militia forward during the fighting at Quatre Bras. Painting by Jan Willem Pienneman. (Rijksmuseum, Amsterdam)

the tiny sheep-farm of La Bergerie towards the crossroads. Lieutenant-Colonel Jan Westenberg, the commanding officer, shouted words of encouragement to try and steady his men, which were followed by an act of great gallantry. The Hereditary Prince of Orange-Nassau placed himself at the head of the battalion, and waving his hat in the air and calling to the troops, he led them forward.

Meanwhile, the 8th Militia Battalion had been forced to withdraw from its position on the extreme right in front of the Bois de Bossu, due to the fierce cannonade to which it was subjected from a

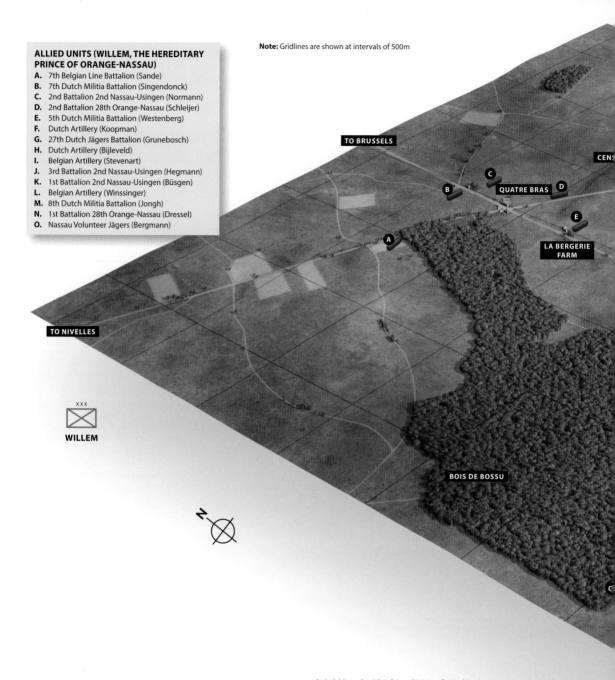

ALLIED UNITS (WILLEM, THE HEREDITARY PRINCE OF ORANGE-NASSAU)

- **A.** 7th Belgian Line Battalion (Sande)
- **B.** 7th Dutch Militia Battalion (Singendonck)
- **C.** 2nd Battalion 2nd Nassau-Usingen (Normann)
- **D.** 2nd Battalion 28th Orange-Nassau (Schleijer)
- **E.** 5th Dutch Militia Battalion (Westenberg)
- **F.** Dutch Artillery (Koopman)
- **G.** 27th Dutch Jägers Battalion (Grunebosch)
- **H.** Dutch Artillery (Bijleveld)
- **I.** Belgian Artillery (Stevenart)
- **J.** 3rd Battalion 2nd Nassau-Usingen (Hegmann)
- **K.** 1st Battalion 2nd Nassau-Usingen (Büsgen)
- **L.** Belgian Artillery (Winssinger)
- **M.** 8th Dutch Militia Battalion (Jongh)
- **N.** 1st Battalion 28th Orange-Nassau (Dressel)
- **O.** Nassau Volunteer Jägers (Bergmann)

Note: Gridlines are shown at intervals of 500m

TO BRUSSELS

CENS

QUATRE BRAS

LA BERGERIE FARM

TO NIVELLES

XXX
WILLEM

N

BOIS DE BOSSU

C

▼ EVENTS

1. At 2:00pm Maréchal Ney ordered the attack to commence upon the crossroads, with the aim of seizing Quatre Bras. The 5th and 9th Infantry Divisions under Baron Bachelu and Comte Foy, with support from the 2nd Cavalry Division commanded by Comte Piré, were given this task. The Netherlands and Nassau troops who held the Bois de Bossu were assailed by a preliminary artillery bombardment, while the French infantry advanced in two columns by battalion. The 2nd Brigade of the 9th Infantry Division, commanded in person by Comte Foy, advanced towards Gémioncourt, driving the Allied skirmishers back, while the 1st Brigade was held in reserve on the heights at Lairalle.

2. At 2.30pm the 5th Infantry Division, flanked by the *chasseurs à cheval* of Comte Piré's 2nd Cavalry Division, marched across the ravine between Gémioncourt and the hamlet of Piraumont. The French artillery moved up and bombarded the Netherlands and Nassau troops deployed along the edge of the Bois de Bossu. Two of the guns belonging to Captain Stevenart's battery were disabled and abandoned and the remaining guns retired, along with the guns commanded by Captain Bijleveld. These took interim positions halfway between Gémioncourt and La Bergerie, close to the high road.

3. At 2.45pm the 5th Dutch Militia Battalion advanced the centre and flank companies in an attempt to secure Gémioncourt. The 27th Dutch Jägers also fortified themselves around the farm, as the 2nd Brigade of the 9th Infantry Division threw out a cloud of *tirailleurs*, who moved towards the farm complex using the high corn as cover. These troops were followed by the three battalions of the 4e Régiment Léger.

THE OPENING SHOTS

The situation at Quatre Bras, 2:00pm, 16 June 1815

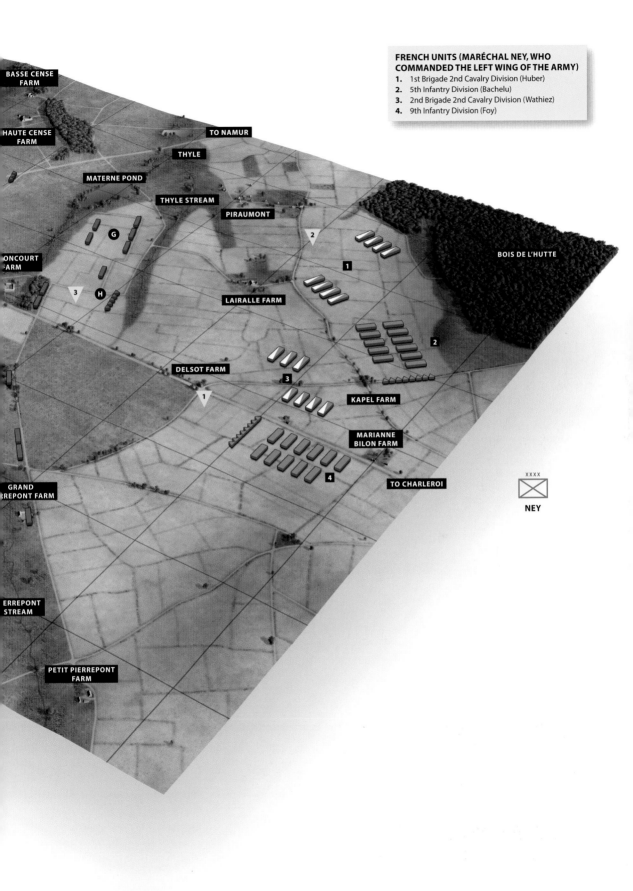

FRENCH UNITS (MARÉCHAL NEY, WHO
COMMANDED THE LEFT WING OF THE ARMY)

1. 1st Brigade 2nd Cavalry Division (Huber)
2. 5th Infantry Division (Bachelu)
3. 2nd Brigade 2nd Cavalry Division (Wathiez)
4. 9th Infantry Division (Foy)

BASSE CENSE
FARM

HAUTE CENSE
FARM

TO NAMUR

THYLE

MATERNE POND

THYLE STREAM

PIRAUMONT

ONCOURT
ARM

G

LAIRALLE FARM

H

BOIS DE L'HUTTE

DELSOT FARM

KAPEL FARM

MARIANNE
BILON FARM

GRAND
REPONT FARM

TO CHARLEROI

xxxx

NEY

ERREPONT
STREAM

PETIT PIERREPONT
FARM

45

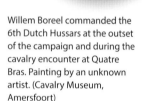

French battery situated on the heights close to the farm of Delsot. The Allied artillery was withdrawn because of the heavy losses it had sustained and the continued threat from the vastly superior French cannon. Captain Emanuel Stevenart, who commanded the battery of foot artillery, was killed and the remaining officers and men encountered tremendous difficulty in moving the guns back to a position on the left of the crossroads along the road to Namur.

The battery of horse artillery also withdrew to a position closer to Quatre Bras.

Throughout this period Prince Bernhard von Sachsen-Weimar had remained in reserve to the right of the Bois de Bossu with the 1st Battalion 28th Orange-Nassau, where he had been joined by the 7th Militia Battalion. But as the French *tirailleurs* encroached he was compelled to detach two companies to skirmish with them and to stop them forcing a passage into the wood. Together with the Nassau Volunteer Jägers and the troops of the 1st Battalion 2nd Nassau-Usingen, the Allied skirmishers were able to maintain the line along the edge of the wood, but they were also subjected to an incessant artillery barrage from the French guns on the heights at Delsot.

With their attacks having gained success the French 4e Régiment Léger occupied the farm of Gémioncourt, while the 100e Régiment de Ligne took a position immediately to the rear of the complex. Together the two battalions covered the movements of the 5th Division, which formed in columns by battalion and advanced towards Quatre Bras. The 6e Chasseurs à Cheval and 5e Lanciers supported this movement, and the vigour of the attack brought the cavalry into the path of the 5th Militia Battalion once again. This time the French horsemen were able to cause considerable disorder, and the movement was turned into a complete rout. The Hereditary Prince of Orange-Nassau narrowly escaped being taken prisoner by the 5e Lanciers, by seeking refuge with two companies of the 7th Line Battalion. However, the French cavalry pursued the debris of the 5th Militia towards the Allied line with malicious fervour.

The Duke of Wellington returned to Quatre Bras as the vanguard of Sir Thomas Picton's 5th Division reached the crossroads, and he immediately dispatched the veteran British troops of the 1st Battalion 95th Regiment of Foot to secure the left of the Allied line and the vulnerable village of Thyle. The green-clad soldiers armed with Baker rifles, under the command of Sir Andrew Barnard, marched along the road to Namur and extended into the fields to the north of Piraumont to prevent the French from making any further progress in this direction.

Fortunately for the duke, reinforcements continued to arrive. Moreover, as the Dutch fell back towards the crossroads, Wellington ordered Picton's men to march along the road to Namur and to lie in the ditches, where they would be sheltered from the French artillery fire emanating from the guns posted between Gémioncourt and Piraumont.

Willem Boreel commanded the 6th Dutch Hussars at the outset of the campaign and during the cavalry encounter at Quatre Bras. Painting by an unknown artist. (Cavalry Museum, Amersfoort)

The Prince of Orange-Nassau leads the Netherlands troops into the fray. The charge by the 6th Dutch Hussars was thrown back in disorder by the 6e Chasseurs à cheval and the French cavalry subsequently overran the artillery at the crossroads. Painting by Reinier Vinkeles. (Rijksmuseum, Amsterdam)

The fighting at Gémioncourt, 3:00pm, 16 June 1815

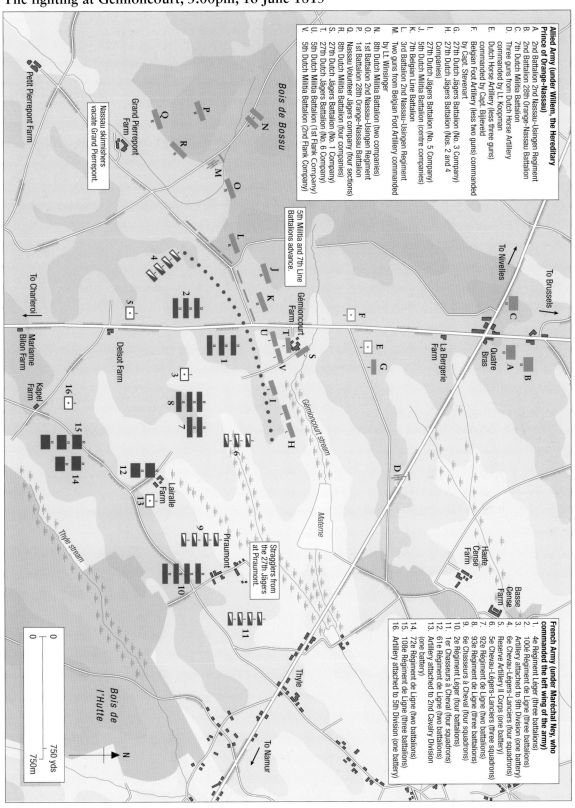

Allied Army (under Willem, the Hereditary Prince of Orange-Nassau)

A. 2nd Battalion 2nd Nassau-Usingen Regiment
B. 2nd Battalion 28th Orange-Nassau Battalion
C. 2nd Battalion 28th Orange-Nassau Battalion
D. 7th Dutch Militia Battalion
E. Three guns from Dutch Horse Artillery commanded by Lt. Koopman
F. Dutch Horse Artillery (less three guns) commanded by Capt. Bijleveld
G. Belgian Foot Artillery (less two guns) commanded by Capt. Stevenart
H. 27th Dutch Jägers Battalion (Nos. 2 and 4 Companies)
J. 27th Dutch Jägers Battalion (No. 5 Company)
K. 27th Dutch Jägers Battalion (centre companies)
L. 7th Belgian Line Battalion
M. Two guns from Belgian Foot Artillery commanded by Lt. Winsinger
N. 8th Dutch Militia Battalion
O. 1st Battalion 2nd Nassau-Usingen Regiment
P. 1st Battalion 28th Orange-Nassau Battalion
Q. Nassau Volunteer Jägers company (four sections)
R. 8th Dutch Militia Battalion (four companies)
S. 27th Dutch Jägers Battalion (No. 1 Company)
T. 27th Dutch Jägers Battalion (No. 6 Company)
U. 5th Dutch Militia Battalion (1st Flank Company)
V. 5th Dutch Militia Battalion (2nd Flank Company)

French Army (under Maréchal Ney, who commanded the left wing of the army)

1. 4e Regiment Léger (three battalions)
2. 100e Regiment de Ligne (three battalions)
3. Artillery attached to 9th Division (one battery)
4. 6e Chevau-Légers-Lanciers (four squadrons)
5. Reserve Artillery II Corps (one battery)
6. 92e Regiment de Ligne (three battalions)
7. 93e Regiment de Ligne (three battalions)
8. 6e Chasseurs à Cheval (four squadrons)
9. 2e Regiment Léger (four battalions)
10. 1er Chasseurs à Cheval (three squadrons)
11. 61e Regiment de Ligne (two battalions)
12. Artillery attached to 2nd Cavalry Division (one battery)
13. 72e Regiment de Ligne (two battalions)
14. 72e Regiment de Ligne (two battalions)
15. 108e Regiment de Ligne (three battalions)
16. Artillery attached to 5th Division (one battery)

Petit Pierrepont Farm

Bois de Bossu

Grand Pierrepont Farm

Nassau skirmishers vacate Grand Pierrepont.

To Nivelles

To Brussels

To Charleroi

5th Militia and 7th Line Battalions advance.

Gémioncourt Farm

Quatre Bras

La Bergerie Farm

Marianne Bilon Farm

Delsot Farm

Gémioncourt stream

Kapel Farm

Materne

Haute Cense Farm

Lairalle Farm

Stragglers from the 27th Jägers at Piraumont.

Piraumont

Basse Cense Farm

Thyle stream

Thyle

To Namur

Bois de l'Hutte

N

0   750 yds
0   750m

Dutch *carabiniers* are shown engaged with French *cuirassiers* during the struggle for the crossroads. No such engagement took place at Quatre Bras, although the two bodies undoubtedly met later in the campaign at Mont St Jean. Painting by Adolphe Lalauze. (Nationaal Militair Museum (NMM) Soesterberg)

The contest at Quatre Bras had been raging for more than an hour when the light cavalry brigade commanded by Baron Jean-Baptiste van Merlen reached the crossroads and were deployed on the left of the high road to Charleroi, with the half-battery of horse artillery under Captain Adriaan Geij. They were the first of the Allied cavalry to reach the battlefield, and having ridden a considerable distance in the oppressive heat, both men and horses were tired. Yet they were given little respite.

The Hereditary Prince of Orange-Nassau immediately rode across to Baron van Merlen and hurriedly ordered him to stem the French tide. The task was bestowed upon Lieutenant-Colonel Willem Boreel and the 6th Dutch Hussars. With insufficient time to form, they charged and collided with the 6e Chasseurs à Cheval north of Gémioncourt. The Dutch cavalry were thrown back and suffered heavy losses. The 5th Belgian Light Dragoons entered the fray, but they too were driven back and retired in confusion towards the crossroads. The disorderly retreat was covered by the 92nd Regiment of Foot, who subjected the enemy cavalry to a devastating volley. But the French horsemen continued into the artillery situated on the high road and passed rapidly between the houses at Quatre Bras. They overran the guns belonging to Captain Stevenart's foot artillery battery and threw themselves upon those commanded by Captain Geij. The French cavalry sabred the officers and men, who crept beneath the cannon for protection, and tested their swords upon the horses belonging to the artillery teams, before they were themselves repulsed.

During the course of the various attacks the French had advanced on all fronts and had almost reached the road to Namur, which linked the Allied Army with the Prussians at Sombreffe. The situation at Quatre Bras was perilous for the Duke of Wellington.

The Duke of Wellington escaped the clutches of the French cavalry that reached the crossroads by seeking shelter with the 92nd (Gordon Highlanders) Regiment of Foot. Painting by Robert Hillingford (Gordon Highlanders Museum, Aberdeen)

ENGAGEMENTS AT QUATRE BRAS AND SOMBREFFE

Napoleon joined the main body of the French Army, which was concentrating at Fleurus, shortly before midday, and, having made a detailed reconnaissance of the area and the opposing force, was convinced that he merely faced a single army corps. He mistakenly believed that this was the rearguard of the Prussian Army, which was retiring north towards the Rhine. At 2:00pm he dictated a short message to Maréchal Soult for Ney at Quatre Bras, informing him that an attack would be made by the wing assigned to Maréchal Grouchy on the enemy between Sombreffe and Brye and that Ney was to repulse the Allied troops before him and wheel to the right so as to envelop the right flank of the Prussian force. However, if the latter were defeated first, the emperor would manoeuvre in the direction of Quatre Bras. Accordingly, shortly after 3:00pm the fighting began in the villages at Ligny and St Amand.

Feldmarschall Blücher and the Prussian general staff had gladly accepted battle, rather than retire to an alternative position further north, despite the fact that they knew that IV Korps commanded by General Bülow, Graf von Dennewitz, would not join them until the following day. This was because they anticipated support from the Allied Army concentrating at Quatre Bras, which they believed had been agreed during the meeting with the Duke of Wellington at the windmill of Bussy at Brye. But when the duke returned to the crossroads he found that the French occupied Piraumont and the farm of Gémioncourt, and that they had pushed back the Netherlands troops in the centre.

Shortly thereafter, Sir James Kempt was ordered to advance into the fields of tall wheat on the left wing with the remaining battalions of the 8th British Brigade, comprising the 28th, 32nd and 79th Regiments of Foot, while Sir Dennis Pack moved into the adjacent fields of rye, closer to the high road to Charleroi, with the 1st, 42nd and 44th Regiments of Foot from the 9th Brigade. The 92nd Regiment of Foot remained in its position by the road as the officers and men of the 5th Division advanced towards the French columns commanded by Baron Bachelu.

The Hanoverian *Landwehr* battalions belonging to the 4th Brigade under Colonel Carl Best, who had been attached temporarily to the 5th Division, were now moved forward next to the road to Namur. The Verden Battalion was deployed into position by Sir Thomas Picton personally, while the marksmen from the brigade formed a chain of skirmishers on the slope of the heights. The Osterode and Münden battalions moved into a narrow meadow lined with a high hedge at a slight angle with the road. This position offered the battalions cover from the enemy fire, although the hedges and crops hindered their view of the terrain in front. The Lüneburg Landwehr Battalion was held in reserve. At this time the 2nd Hanoverian Foot Artillery battery commanded by Captain Carl von Rettberg unlimbered in a position on the left of the farmhouse at Quatre Bras and immediately opened fire upon the enemy.

In the Bois de Bossu the fighting intensified. The French *tirailleurs* forced their way into the wood above the left flank of the 1st Battalion 28th Orange-Nassau Regiment, and the troops commanded by Prince Bernhard von Sachsen-Weimar were gradually driven back to a position close to a small stream. The undergrowth and thick smoke from the muskets ensured that the fighting became increasingly confused, as with the exception of the company of Volunteer Jägers, who had expended almost all of their ammunition in the

THE CLASH BETWEEN THE DUTCH-BELGIAN AND FRENCH LIGHT CAVALRY (PP. 50–51)

The brigade of light cavalry commanded by Major-General Baron Jean-Baptiste van Merlen reached Quatre Bras towards 3:30pm. It comprised the 6th Dutch Hussars Regiment, numbering over 640 officers and men in four squadrons, under the command of Lieutenant-Colonel Willem Boreel, and the 5th Belgian Light Dragoons Regiment, with over 440 officers and men in three squadrons, commanded by Lieutenant-Colonel Édouard de Mercx. They took a position on the left of the crossroads, in rear of the artillery, which was covered by a line of skirmishers. The cavalry had hardly moved into position when the Prince of Orange-Nassau ordered Baron van Merlen to charge two regiments of French *chasseurs à cheval*, which had advanced close to the high road leading from Charleroi to Brussels. The 6th Dutch Hussars, being the foremost of the two Allied cavalry regiments, was ordered to advance. The 1st Squadron, which was standing in column, attempted to form before being led forward, however, the haste in which the movement took place meant this process was not completed. The Dutch horsemen advanced at the full trot, followed consecutively by their comrades in the three other squadrons. Having closed upon the French cavalry the order to

charge was given, and the leading company came into contact with the enemy. The 6th Hussars **(1)**, wearing blue tunics, were engaged with the 6e Régiment de Chasseurs à Cheval **(2)**, clad in their famous green uniforms, from the brigade commanded by Maréchal-de-camp Baron Pierre-François Huber. The French numbered 550 officers and men in four squadrons, under Colonel Paul-Eugène de Faudouas. Both the 1er and 6e Régiments de Chasseurs à Cheval had trotted forward in perfect order towards the crossroads, supported by a body of *tirailleurs*. The initial impact of the charge forced the 6e Chasseurs back, but the 6th Hussars were unable to take advantage of this success, and as the remaining French squadrons moved up, the Allied cavalry was forced to retire. The 5th Belgian Light Dragons had also been ordered into the fray, but they were unable to stop the rearward movement, as the 6th Hussars rode back through the artillery in the direction of the buildings at Quatre Bras, followed closely by the French cavalry. The *chasseurs* overran the guns, and were only driven off by the accurate fire from the 92nd Regiment of Foot, which lined a nearby ditch.

contest, neither the Nassau nor the Netherlands soldiers defending the wood were experienced at manoeuvring as light infantry in extended order. Prince Bernhard sent urgent word to the Hereditary Prince of Orange-Nassau that suitable reinforcements were required. Fortunately, the first of the Brunswick contingent had begun to arrive at Quatre Bras, including the two companies of rifle-armed Grey Jägers of the Avantgarde, who were sent to support their beleaguered allies in the Bois de Bossu.

The Brunswick troops skirmish with the French between the Bois de Bossu and the high road. The Grey Jägers of the Avantagarde are on the left of the scene. Painting by Richard Knötel. (Landesmuseum, Braunschweig)

As the Brunswick troops reached the field of battle they were thrown into the action. The 2nd Light Battalion under Major Heinrich von Brandenstein was promptly detached in the direction of Piraumont, to occupy the Bois des Cense. The two light companies of the Avantgarde, clad in black and armed with muskets, along with the Leib and 1st Line battalions, moved to positions south of the crossroads, between the high road and the Bois de Bossu, where the former could communicate with their rifle-armed compatriots in the wood. The 2nd Line Battalion and the Uhlans took positions a little further to the rear, while the Duke of Brunswick led the Hussars along the road to Namur to where the battery commanded by Brevet Major Thomas Rogers had been unlimbered. The duke smoked calmly on his pipe and rode up and down in front of the young cavalrymen, as the balls from a French horse artillery battery posted beyond the Materne pond flew menacingly overhead.

PICTON COUNTERATTACKS WITH THE 5TH DIVISION

The heat was unbearable and the dust from the crops made the officers and men of Sir Thomas Picton's 5th Division choke as they fought their way through the fields towards the French columns between Gémioncourt and Piraumont. The stalks of wheat and rye were so tall that those on foot were unable to see their enemy, and it was impossible to maintain order under such circumstances. Eventually, the straggling line emerged into the open fields of grass beyond.

On the right, closest to the high road, was the 42nd Regiment of Foot or 'Black Watch', as the highland Scots were more commonly known. On the extreme left, adjacent to the farm and hamlet of Piraumont, were their highland countrymen in the 79th. Their sudden appearance revealed the close proximity of the French infantry, and they were instantly assailed by a hail of fire as they attempted to restore order to the ranks. Dutch troops now passed hurriedly between the regiments in their flight from the field. These were stragglers from the 27th Jägers and 5th Militia battalions. Without a moment to consider the consequences, Sir Thomas Picton took the bold course of action and ordered those on the right to fire a single volley and to charge the enemy with bayonets fixed. The air was immediately filled with thick smoke and the cries of war, as the British attacked their adversaries with unguarded zeal.

Picton sent word for the 79th to advance on the left, so as to cover the flank of the three battalions that were involved in the attack, and for the 28th and 32nd Regiments to form as a reserve in the rear. The Light Company, together with No 8 Company, were thrown forward from the 79th Regiment to skirmish with the French *tirailleurs*, while the remainder of the battalion advanced at the double.

The 2e Régiment Léger formed the head of Baron Bachelu's Division, as it had since the first morning of the campaign. The officers and men had demonstrated their customary valour and driven the thin line of Dutch soldiers from the field of battle in confusion as they advanced in column towards the crossroads. But the suddenness and vigour of the attack by the men of the 42nd Regiment caused them to hesitate momentarily. This was enough to afford the Scots the opportunity to fire and charge. The French fell back towards Piraumont where they re-formed. It was now their turn to commence a violent fusillade against the highland troops, which was supported by the artillery attached to the division. The men of the 42nd Regiment, who had pursued so vigorously, felt the full force of the French salvo, and within minutes the ground was littered with their bodies.

While the encounter escalated, the *chasseurs à cheval* and *lanciers* commanded by Comte Piré advanced, using the undulations in the terrain and the height of the crops to cover their movement. When they appeared from the low ground and charged the left flank, the three British battalions formed square so remarkably that they were unable to launch a serious attack and were repelled. The ensuing volleys from the British squares sent a considerable number of cavalrymen crashing to the ground. However, exposed as they were in the open fields to the continued threat from the enemy infantry, artillery and cavalry, the 42nd, along with the 44th and 1st Regiments, who were a little to the rear, were ordered to retire to their former positions.

Sir Thomas Picton had ridden forward with the British troops as they attacked the head of the French column. Although mounted on horseback, he was less conspicuous than many Allied officers as he wore a blue frock-coat buttoned to the collar, dark trousers, boots and a large round hat. But unbeknown to the men of the 5th Division, it was now that he was struck a glancing blow from a spent cannonball. The injury was severe, but the courageous Welshman did not disclose the nature of the wound to his subordinates and remained with his division to animate the troops throughout the course of the day.

The situation facing the wounded men leaving the battlefield to seek medical attention was becoming increasingly difficult. Most were treated on the side of the road leading from Quatre Bras to

Sir James Kempt commanded the 8th British Brigade, composed of veteran officers and men. The brigade was part of the 5th Division under Sir Thomas Picton. Painting by Robert McInnes. (Royal Collection Trust, © Her Majesty Queen Elizabeth II, 2014 / Bridgeman Images)

Nivelles, which was already heavily congested with ammunition and baggage wagons. Once they had been bandaged, those belonging to the 2nd Netherlands Division that were able to walk were directed to make their way to the market square in Nivelles, as the field hospital had been established in the town hall. The seriously wounded were placed in carts for transportation, although this was a slow, painful journey in the circumstances. Further north, on the road to Brussels, the British, Hanoverian and Brunswick surgeons had prepared a temporary hospital in the last of the buildings at Quatre Bras, and were beginning to receive the first of the wounded men from their respective contingents. But even here they were not immune to the force of the French cannonade.

The Duke of Wellington was acutely aware of the imbalance in the contest between the Allied and French artillery. Captain Rettberg's battery of Hanoverian foot artillery, which was located on the left of Quatre Bras, the British battery commanded by Brevet Major Rogers, which was positioned on the road to Namur, along with the remaining three guns from Captain Bijleveld's Dutch horse artillery, under the temporary command of Second Lieutenant Wijnand Koopman, which were covering the Namur road, were all the duke had to call upon, for the remainder of the Netherlands artillery had suffered in the contest and had withdrawn to various positions behind Quatre Bras. Consequently, the duke summoned Sir George Wood, commanding the British artillery, and ordered him to send word to the artillery batteries en route to the crossroads to make haste, so as to reinforce their hard-pressed comrades.

FORCED MARCHES TO THE BATTLEFIELD AT QUATRE BRAS

Having been dispersed in such wide cantonments, the various divisions within the Allied Army had a considerable distance to march in order to reach the crossroads. The Duke of Wellington's order to move upon Braine-le-Comte had reached the headquarters of the 1st Division in Enghien at 1:30am that morning, and after somewhat lengthy preliminaries the 2nd Guards Brigade and the 2nd Battalion 1st Foot Guards marched from their billets within the environs of the château. The 3rd Battalion 1st Foot Guards were quartered in Hove and Marcq; they joined the division en route, and together the troops marched along the winding roads and across the former battlefield of Steenkirk. The heat of the day was already oppressive, and the Guards were glad to reach their destination at 9:00am.

Major-General George Cooke, who commanded the division, ordered the troops to halt in the fields to the east of the town, and sent his aide-de-camp to the Hereditary Prince

A contemporary portrayal of the fighting at Quatre Bras based upon accounts of the battle. Coloured aquatint by William Heath (National Army Museum, London / Bridgeman Images)

The Régiments d'Infanterie Léger from within the II Corps played an extensive part in the fighting at Quatre Bras, particularly in the Bois de Bossu and at Piraumont. Print by Martinet. (Bibliothèque Nationale de France, Paris)

Friedrich Wilhelm, Duke of Brunswick is shown leading the Brunswick Hussars in a gallant charge during the fighting at Quatre Bras. Coloured aquatint by William Heath. (Anne SK Brown Military Collection, Rhode Island)

of Orange-Nassau's headquarters, which was located at the Hôtel du Miroir, for further instructions. Captain George Disbrowe made his way through the crowded streets, but there were no orders awaiting the division at the hotel. Upon being informed of this fact, Major-General Cooke rode south to make a reconnaissance and to gather intelligence. He returned at midday, determined to continue the march, and with the artillery and the 1st Brigade at the head of the column, the Guards moved along the paved road towards Nivelles.

The 3rd Division, commanded by Lieutenant-General Count Carl von Alten, had already passed through Soignies, Braine-le-Comte and Nivelles in its march to the crossroads at Quatre Bras. The weary troops rested for a short time on the side of the road close to Nivelles, but the sound of the guns in the distance encouraged Count von Alten to proceed without further delay. Captain Andreas Cleeves of the King's German Legion was ordered to move forward of the division in the direction of Houtain-le-Val with the battery of horse artillery that he commanded, and it was here that he received the order from the Duke of Wellington to hasten to the field of battle.

The duke and his staff were standing in front of the farmhouse at the crossroads when Cleeves and his men arrived, and so he immediately reported to Sir George Wood. The battery was positioned on the right of the line and began to fire 8-pound shells, in which there were 35 small balls, in an attempt to disperse a body of enemy cavalry. But after a short time Sir George Wood ordered Cleeves to move 500 paces along the road to Namur, and fire upon an enemy battery positioned in front of Piraumont which was doing great execution with its oblique fire. After a brisk trot along the road, the guns were unlimbered close to the Hanoverian battery commanded by Captain von Rettberg, and unleashed upon the enemy.

It was approaching 4:00pm and most of the Brunswick contingent had reached the battlefield, although the artillery and the 1st and 3rd light battalions were still absent. The Duke of Wellington personally ordered Duke Friedrich Wilhelm to send one of his staff officers back on the high road to Brussels to hasten their arrival. Furthermore, the Hussars were ordered to move across the field, to join with the remainder of the corps. The Leib Battalion, along with the 1st Line Battalion and the two light companies of the Avantgarde advanced along the road and took a position between La Bergerie and the stream which ran into the wood. A skirmish line was extended to the front and right in order to make contact with the Allied troops defending the Bois de Bossu. The Hussars and the Uhlans formed in rear of these troops, while the 2nd and 3rd line battalions were positioned close to Quatre Bras as a reserve to cover the possible withdrawal of those in the front line.

Jérôme Bonaparte's 6th Division was the last of those from II Corps that bivouacked in Gosselies to set out on the road towards Frasnes. As the troops marched along the high road they heard the cannonade from Fleurus on their right, and shortly thereafter the unmistakeable music of the guns at Quatre Bras was clear. The officers and men of the 1er Régiment Léger had the honour of leading the column onto the field of battle, and they arrived at the same time as Napoleon's 2:00pm order was delivered to Maréchal Ney by Charles, Comte de Forbin-Janson.

Ney immediately placed himself at the head of the regiment and sent word to Comte Piré to support his attack with the cavalry. A battery of horse artillery was directed onto the heights to the west of Gémioncourt, in order to fire at the Brunswick battalions that had moved into an advanced position between the Bois de Bossu and the high road to Charleroi. The French marshal led the three battalions of the regiment across the field towards the Bois de Bossu, and here the French *tirailleurs* gradually overpowered the Allied skirmishers, who had regained some of the ground they had lost earlier in the day. The 2nd Battalion of the 1er Régiment Léger advanced into the wood, while the 1st and 3rd battalions were held in reserve.

Another depiction of the charge by the Brunswick Hussars against the French infantry occupying the farm of La Bergerie. The Duke of Brunswick is shown in the centre and has just received his mortal wound. Coloured aquatint by Charles Warren. (Anne SK Brown Military Collection, Rhode Island)

THE GALLANT DEMISE OF THE DUKE OF BRUNSWICK

The Brunswick Leib and 1st Line Battalions suffered severely from the relentless French artillery barrage, as did the other battalions. Major Friedrich von Cramm of the Hussars was killed, while Major Adolph von Rauschenplatt of the Avantegarde was severely wounded, losing his left arm. But they maintained their ground in the face of the terrible onslaught for some considerable time.

Friedrich Wilhelm, Duke of Brunswick receives his mortal wound. The Bois de Bossu can be seen on the left, with the buildings and crossroads of Quatre Bras visible in the distance. Coloured aquatint by Franz Manskirch. (British Library, London)

From his advanced position, Maréchal Ney ordered Jérôme Bonaparte to move against the vulnerable Brunswick squares with the two battalions of the 3e Régiment de Ligne. The Duke of Brunswick perceived the attack by the two French columns and ordered the Hussars, which were hindered by the terrain

THE DEPLOYMENT OF THE ARTILLERY BATTERY UNDER CAPTAIN CLEEVES (PP. 58–59)

The disparity between the accurate and powerful French artillery and that employed in the defence of Quatre Bras by 4:00pm forced the Duke of Wellington to send riders back on the roads with messages for the batteries en route to the crossroads to advance with the utmost haste. Shortly after 4:00pm the horse artillery battery designated as No 4 Company King's German Legion, comprising five officers and over 200 men, armed with five 9-pdr guns and one 5½in. howitzer, reached the battlefield. As the duke and his staff were stationed in front of the farmhouse, Captain Andreas Cleeves (1), who commanded the battery, immediately reported to the senior artillery officer, Sir George Wood. He was ordered to unlimber on the right of the line and to fire 8-pound shells at a body of enemy cavalry. This was undertaken with remarkable precision. However, the battery was subsequently ordered to move some 500 paces along the Namur road, and to fire upon an enemy battery positioned in front of Piraumont, which was inflicting considerable damage on the Allied troops in this area with its oblique fire. The guns were re-harnessed to the teams and the artillerymen clambered onto the limbers in a most unusual manner, to facilitate the speedy manoeuvre of the battery along the road. As the guns trotted passed the various Hanoverian battalions belonging to the 4th Brigade, commanded by Colonel Best, which lined the ditches and hedges to the north of the high road, the men exchanged messages. But on approaching the point of the road adjacent to the hamlet of Piraumont, the battery came under heavy fire. Most of the balls fell short of the road, lodging in the ditches and throwing mud into the air. But a number found their target, killing and severely wounding several of the drivers and artillerymen. The guns belonging to the 2nd Hanoverian artillery battery commanded by Captain Carl von Rettberg (2) were already deployed at this point and actively engaged with the enemy. The soldiers were delighted to see their fellow countrymen. Captain Cleeves immediately gave the order for his guns to move off the road onto the small plateau to the south, and to unlimber close to the Hanoverian battery. Once the two units were united their combined firepower silenced the French guns and allowed the Allied infantry to advance from their concealed positions into the open fields.

and the close proximity of the wood, to retire onto the other side of the road towards Quatre Bras. He collected the Uhlans and charged the enemy, but the attack failed completely, due to the strength and composure of the French infantry. The Uhlans were staggered by a tremendous volley, and were themselves compelled to retreat towards Quatre Bras.

A sizeable body of *dragons* (which many of the Allied troops mistook for *cuirassiers*) from the reserve cavalry corps commanded by Comte Valmy now advanced along the high road and threatened the two Brunswick infantry battalions. As the enemy force was vastly superior in strength, Duke Friedrich Wilhelm ordered the two battalions to retire while formed in square. The 1st Line Battalion moved back towards the crossroads, but the Leib Battalion, under the command of Major Friedrich von Pröstler, with whom the duke was stationed, positioned itself on the left of La Bergerie. The Brunswick troops executed this movement as slowly and as well as possible under the violent cannonade. But the impact of the cannonballs and the subsequent advance of the *dragons* created momentary panic within the battalion. The duke attempted to restore order, and as he rode unaccompanied outside of the square to rally the men, he was mortally wounded by a musket ball which passed through his left wrist and into his abdomen.

Duke Friedrich Wilhelm collapsed to the ground on the right side of his horse, halfway between the Brunswick square and the enemy column. Seeing their stricken leader fall, several men ran forward. Lifting him as carefully as they could, they carried the duke in a blanket to the Namur road, where he spoke briefly before his death to Major Friedrich von Wachholtz, the adjutant-general, and the command of the Brunswick Corps passed to Colonel Elias Olfermann.

Despite the loss of their beloved duke the various Brunswick battalions re-formed to the rear of the buildings at Quatre Bras, where they awaited the arrival of the 1st and 3rd light battalions and the artillery under the command of Major Carl von Moll. The Allied guns posted along the heights continued to fire upon the enemy. However, the French were inspired and they advanced with renewed courage towards the crossroads.

Members of the Leib Battalion are shown carrying the Duke of Brunswick to the rear. The sheep farm of La Bergerie can be seen clearly on the left of the scene. Painting by Heinrich Monten. (Landesmuseum, Braunschweig)

A CONCERTED FRENCH ATTACK UPON THE CROSSROADS

Maréchal Ney encouraged the troops of Jérôme Bonaparte's 6th Division, who were under his personal guidance, as they moved forward. The 1st Brigade, commanded by Baron Pierre-François Bauduin, was fully engaged in the attack on the left of the French line. The 2nd Battalion of the 1er Régiment

Léger had marched into the Bois de Bossu behind a cloud of *tirailleurs*, while the 1st and 3rd battalions of the regiment remained on the edge of the wood. The two battalions of the 3e Régiment de Ligne were formed in column and were advancing between the wood and the high road to Charleroi. The 2nd Brigade, under the command of Baron Jean-Louis Soye, was positioned in reserve to the south, adjacent to the farms of Grand and Petit Pierrepoint.

In the centre, the ground immediately around Gémioncourt was held by the infantry of Baron Jean-Baptiste Jamin's 2nd Brigade from Comte Foy's 9th Division, while the two regiments of *dragons* belonging to Baron Samuel-François l'Heritier's 11th Cavalry Division trotted menacingly forward on the high road. On the opposite side of the road, between Gémioncourt and Piraumont, were the guns attached to the 9th Division, and to the south, on the heights at Delsot, were the troops of Baron Jean-Joseph Gauthier's Brigade and the reserve artillery.

Comte Piré had originally been directed to the right, where the terrain was very difficult for cavalry to manoeuvre, and so he was called back to the centre and left to act under Maréchal Ney's immediate orders. However, the battery of horse artillery attached to the 2nd Cavalry Division remained close to the Materne pond. Some 500 paces to the rear of the guns were the 72e and 108e Régiments de Ligne from Baron Bachelu's 5th Division, with whom Comte Reille and his staff were positioned.

On the right, the four battalions of the 2e Régiment Léger were deployed at Piraumont and in the fields immediately to the fore. Behind the farm complex, acting as a reserve and covering the divisional artillery, were the two battalions of the 61e Régiment de Ligne. The 7th Division, commanded by Baron Jean-Baptiste Girard, was not present as it had been detached from the II Corps, and was embroiled in the heavy fighting in and around the village of St Amand.

The Lanciers Rouges of the Garde Impériale had been kept in reserve at Frasnes along with the two batteries of horse artillery which had accompanied them, and had not been committed to the contest, in accordance with the emperor's wishes. They were joined in the vicinity of the small village by the 8e and 11e Régiments de Cuirassiers from Comte Valmy's III Reserve Cavalry Corps. However, the *carabiniers* and *cuirassiers* from the 12th Cavalry Division were with the emperor at Fleurus. Together with the various divisions of Comte d'Erlon's I Corps, they constituted a sizeable part of Maréchal Ney's command which was yet to reach the battlefield.

To the east of the high road the six squadrons of the Brunswick Hussars had reformed under the command of Major Anton von Oeynhausen, and were anxiously watching the approach of the French cavalry. On their right flank were the 2e and 7e Dragons, who had almost reached La Bergerie, while only 1,000 paces from their left were the 5e and 6e Lanciers. The Brunswick Hussars moved to the right, sensing the *dragons* would charge, but as they closed on their

The crossroads at Quatre Bras viewed from the north. The northern tip of the Bois de Bossu is visible on the right of the scene. Coloured aquatint by an unknown English artist (National Army Museum, London / Bridgeman Images)

opponents they were severely raked by the fire from the French artillery posted at Gémioncourt. The shock was absolute, as scores of men and horses fell, and the Hussars were momentarily gripped by fear. Rather than continuing towards the *dragons* they wheeled to the right and began to stream back to the relative safety of the Brunswick infantry battalions posted at the crossroads. But in their flight the Hussars galloped towards the position occupied by the 92nd Regiment of Foot, which lined the ditch to the south of the Namur road.

The *dragons* pressed home their advantage and charged, and a mass of horsemen swept along the high road. Lieutenant-Colonel John Cameron, who commanded the highland regiment, ordered the Grenadier Company to deploy at a right angle to the remainder of the battalion, so as to deliver oblique fire at the enemy cavalry. This manoeuvre was accomplished at the very moment the Duke of Wellington and his staff arrived in rear of the Scots. Wellington instantly gave the command to present arms, and, as the head of the Brunswick cavalry cleared the line, the order to fire followed. The muskets answered in unison, but fortunately for the French *dragons* they had observed the British troops and veered hastily to the left. With the exception of a single officer, who had ridden too far forward of his men, none were killed or wounded, but the momentum of the charge was lost.

Despite this fact the French attack had not been thwarted, for the first of the two dense columns from the 3e Régiment de Ligne had advanced as far as La Bergerie. Sir Edward Barnes, the adjutant-general, was ordered to ride to the extreme right of the 92nd Regiment by the duke to obtain an unobstructed view of the French infantry and its movements. Having hurried across to the right wing, he could see that the enemy had seized the buildings and enclosures of the sheep farm only 300 paces from the crossroads. Judging that action was required immediately, Barnes removed his hat and waving it above his head, called for the highlanders to follow him. Towards the centre of the line the Duke of Wellington, who had been watching closely, turned to Cameron and said: 'Now, Cameron, is your time – take care of that road.' The battalion cleared the ditch and marched at the double onto the road to Charleroi, where the Grenadier and No. 1 companies were formed in column. The remaining companies formed in line slightly to the rear, and the whole advanced rapidly.

Almost as soon as the officers and men of the 92nd Regiment had moved into the open they were assailed by the fire from the French *tirailleurs*. Ensign John McPherson, who carried the Regimental Colour, was killed, but the highland troops pressed on. Within minutes they had driven the enemy back to the farm buildings and the hedges and walls which surrounded the garden. However, the fire emanating from these vantage points was tremendous, and for an instant the Scots wavered. Cameron ordered the two leading companies to advance and passed to the west of the enclosure on the ground adjacent to the high road. Conspicuous on horseback at the forefront of the action, within moments he was mortally wounded by a musket ball which entered his groin, and he slumped forward on his mount. Realizing that their colonel was severely wounded, the Scots poured forth. Sir Augustus Frazer of the Allied horse artillery, who was close at hand, and two

Prince Jérôme Bonaparte was appointed to the command of the 6th Infantry Division within Comte Reille's II Corps. The conduct of the emperor's younger brother became the subject of considerable discussion in the aftermath of the campaign. Painting by Sébastien Weygandt. (Neue Galerie, Kassel, Germany / © Museumslandschaft Hessen Kassel / Ute Brunzel / Bridgeman Images)

soldiers from the regiment escorted the animal back to the crossroads, where Cameron was lowered to the ground. He was attended by his groom and his foster-brother, Ewen Macmillan, before a party of men lifted him gently into a wagon taking the wounded to Genappe.

The loss of their courageous commanding officer provoked the greatest anger amidst the highland soldiers, and they sought to exact full retribution upon their foe. With bayonets fixed, they advanced into the ferocious fusillade with such determination that the French infantry withdrew. This success was gained at a high price however, and the command of the battalion changed hands four times in quick succession before it finally devolved upon Captain Peter Wilkie. Now the depleted ranks were subjected to a violent barrage from the French guns positioned at Gémioncourt, and being isolated from the main line and threatened by the enemy cavalry, the order was given to withdraw into the Bois de Bossu. The highlanders continued to sustain heavy losses, but once the remnants of the battalion reached the haven of the wood, they were able to make their way slowly north towards the road leading to Nivelles.

Sir Edward Barnes exhorted the 92nd (Gordon Highlanders) Regiment of Foot to charge the French infantry which had occupied La Bergerie. Painting by Jack Girbal. (Private collection)

The Chevau-Léger Lanciers belonging to Comte Piré's Cavalry Division were among the most formidable horsemen in Europe. Print by Martinet. (Bibliothèque Nationale de France, Paris)

CAVALRY CHARGES AGAINST THE ALLIED FORMATIONS

While the fighting had been raging around La Bergerie, the British troops belonging to Sir Thomas Picton's 5th Division had gradually withdrawn from their exposed positions towards the road to Namur. The 44th Regiment of Foot had retired to the gentle slope at the foot of the heights, but they now received the order from Sir Denis Pack to advance in line, two-deep, to a point some 200 paces beyond the sheep farm. This was achieved, and they came to a halt with their right flank resting close to the high road to Charleroi. Lieutenant-Colonel George O'Malley, the second-in-command, was riding in rear of the troops alongside Major-General Pack, when he noticed a body of cavalry on the opposite side of the road. The old soldiers of the Grenadier Company, who were the closest to the high road, were convinced that they were French *lanciers*. However, both Pack and O'Malley believed that they were Belgians and the order was issued not to fire upon them.

The beleaguered officers and men of the 42nd Regiment of Foot had also advanced in line to the south-east of La Bergerie, and had emerged into an open field of tall grass overlooking Gémioncourt. The highland troops could see the cavalry approaching from the low ground between the Bois de Bossu and the high road, and immediately raised their concerns to the officers, especially as the skirmishers were detached in extended order. The officers assured the men that the cavalry

The 42nd (Black Watch) Regiment of Foot fight for their lives in a desperate struggle against the French cavalry. Painting by William Wollen (Black Watch Museum, Perth)

were friendly, but a number of the veterans insisted that they were from the 6e Régiment de Chevau-Leger-Lanciers. With the agreement of Lieutenant George Munro, a round was fired to provoke a response, and the cavalry instantly moved towards the battalion's right flank. Any lingering doubt was expelled by a German Dragoon, who came galloping up and exclaimed: 'Franchee! Franchee!', before wheeling about and riding off.

Having remained in line the highland troops were not formed properly to receive enemy cavalry, and so as the skirmishers nearest to the main body of the battalion ran in, shouts rang out to form square. The rear face of the formation was rapidly completed by No 4 and No 5 companies, while the sides of the square were almost in place. But the front face, where the Grenadier and No. 1 companies should have been stationed, was open, as the former had been detached. Indeed, the Grenadier and Light companies were the first to bear the brunt of the cavalry attack.

The officers and men of the Grenadier Company fought for their lives as the *lanciers* burst upon them. Captain Archibald Menzies had chosen to fight on

The 28th (North Gloucestershire) Regiment of Foot are shown in square repelling a charge by the French light cavalry. Painting by Elisabeth Thompson. (National Gallery of Victoria, Melbourne, Australia / Bridgeman Images)

THE ATTACK BY THE 92ND REGIMENT OF FOOT UPON LA BERGERIE (PP. 66–67)

By 4:30pm two dense infantry columns had advanced from the French line as far as the farm of La Bergerie. The columns were formed by the two battalions of the 3e Régiment de Ligne, comprising more than 900 officers and men, and were supported by the cavalry from the 2nd Cavalry Division. They prepared to attack the crossroads. The 92nd Regiment of Foot or Gordon Highlanders were stationed on the left of Quatre Bras, in a ditch which ran to the north of the road to Namur. The Duke of Wellington and his staff rode across and took a position in rear of the famous Scottish troops. Sir Edward Barnes, the adjutant-general, was ordered to the right to obtain an unrestricted view of the French infantry and its movements, which was only 300 paces from the crossroads. Judging that immediate action was required, Barnes waved his hat above his head, and the duke ordered the commander of the regiment, John Cameron, to secure the road. The highlanders cleared the ditch and marched at the double along the road leading south to Charleroi. The regiment comprised almost 700 officers and men. Now the Grenadier and No 1 Companies formed at the front in column, while the remaining companies were in line slightly to the rear.

They advanced rapidly, but were assailed by the *tirailleurs*, who poured accurate fire upon the officers and those holding the Colours. Ensign John McPherson, who carried the Regimental Colour, was killed. But the highlanders marched forward and approached the hedges and walls which surrounded the sheep farm. The musket fire emanating from these points was tremendous, and the Scots momentarily wavered. John Cameron gave the order for the two leading companies to advance to the west of the enclosures. He was conspicuous on horseback, as he rode forward on the ground adjacent to the high road (1), and was subject to close-range *tirailleurs* fire (2). A musket ball struck him in the groin and he slumped forward. Realizing their colonel was hit the highlanders poured forth. Fortunately, Sir Augustus Frazer of the horse artillery was close at hand, and with two soldiers from the 92nd Regiment, he escorted Cameron and the animal back to the crossroads. Here, the wounded colonel was lifted from his mount and placed in a wagon, which was taken to Genappe by his foster brother, Ewen Macmillan. But the wound proved fatal.

foot and was in the midst of the mêlée. He eventually collapsed to the ground covered with wounds. The French horsemen reaped death and misery upon their hapless victims, and continued towards the incomplete square. Recognizing the need to close ranks immediately the order was bellowed for No. 1 and No. 8 companies to wheel back, and thus create an improvised front face. Somehow in the confusion several *lanciers* penetrated into the heart of the formation before the manoeuvre could be finished, and for a moment chaos reigned. But the French were either bayoneted or shot, as no quarter was given.

Sir Robert Macara, who commanded the 42nd Regiment, was wounded during the bitter struggle, and as the fighting had abated somewhat, a party of four men was ordered to wrap him in a blanket and carry him to the rear. They had gone but a short distance when they were ridden down and killed to a man by another squadron of *lanciers*. Like their highland comrades in the 92nd Regiment of Foot, those of the 'Black Watch' had suffered severely in the contest, which was far from over.

In their position close to La Bergerie, the 44th Regiment of Foot had remained in line, as Sir Denis Pack believed that the body of cavalry on the opposite side of the road was composed of Belgians, despite protestations from a considerable number of the men within the ranks. The error of judgement was confirmed, as the 5e Lanciers belonging to Comte Piré's 2nd Cavalry Division rapidly closed upon them. Lieutenant-Colonel John Hamerton, the commanding officer, could see that it would be impossible to form square in sufficient time to repel the attack, and so without any

The officers and men of the 44th (East Essex) Regiment of Foot suffer during another attack upon their square by the French light cavalry. Painting by Vereker Hamilton (Museum of New Zealand, Wellington)

Sir Robert Macara and the party of Grenadiers carrying him to the rear were slain by a body of French *lanciers*. Painting by Richard Simkin (Black Watch Museum, Perth)

Sir Colin Halkett was a Hanoverian officer who served in the British Army during the Peninsular War. In 1815 he was appointed to the command of the 5th British Brigade within Alten's 3rd Division. Painting by Jan Willem Pieneman (Apsley House, The Wellington Museum, London, UK / Bridgeman Images)

hesitation he ordered the rear rank to face about. The order was obeyed smartly and the men stood in two lines back to back.

As the *lanciers* drew near, the men in the rear line levelled their muskets and poured a devastating volley into the cavalry. One particularly determined horseman made a dash for the King's Colour, which was borne by Ensign James Christie. The officer received an appalling wound to his face when the Frenchman lunged forward with his lance, and Christie slumped to the ground, the Colour still in his grasp. Although the gallant *lancier* succeeded in tearing a small triangle of silk from the standard, like many of his fellow countrymen, he paid for his valour with his life. The cavalry was repelled, and retired to the sanctuary of the French line.

Exhausted by their exertions and running short of ammunition, the 42nd and 44th retired slowly to the open ground adjacent to the road to Namur, where they formed a single square. On their left, some 200 paces further forward, the 1st or Royal Scots and the 28th Regiment of Foot did likewise, and they were joined by the highland troops of the 79th, each of the regiments having been obliged to withdraw from their advanced positions. It was approaching 5:00pm and the Allied soldiers were in desperate need of reinforcement.

THE TIMELY INTERVENTION OF THE 3RD DIVISION

Both the officers and men of Sir Colin Halkett's and Count Friedrich von Kielmansegge's brigades suffered during the arduous march to Quatre Bras. The sweltering heat was suffocating, yet there was no opportunity to rest as they approached the field of battle along the crowded road to Nivelles. Count Carl von Alten, who commanded the division to which the brigades belonged, had ridden ahead with his staff and was directed by the Hereditary Prince of Orange-Nassau to deploy the various battalions the moment they reached the crossroads.

At the head of the column was the 30th Regiment of Foot, followed by the 33rd, 69th and the 73rd respectively. As the British troops came up they were ordered to take post in the trampled fields of grass adjacent to the Bois de Bossu. The 30th, 33rd and 73rd executed this order, and joined with the Brunswick Leib, 1st and 2nd line battalions, all of which had advanced a short time before to support the 92nd Regiment of Foot. The 69th Regiment was detached however to the opposite side of the high road, where it took a position slightly to the north of La Bergerie. The battery of foot artillery attached to the 3rd Division, which was commanded by Brevet Major William Lloyd, augmented these movements. Two 9-pdrs were moved forward, to the right of the 69th, while the remaining four guns unlimbered close to the high road, immediately in front of the farm at Quatre Bras.

The troops of the 1st Hanoverian Brigade under Count Friedrich von Kielmansegge now reached the crossroads and were ordered to continue their march along the road to the left flank, so as to reinforce the British and Brunswickers defending this part of the Allied line. The Lüneburg Light Infantry Battalion advanced at the front of the brigade and was subjected to a most galling fire from the French *tirailleurs* belonging to the 2e Régiment Léger. Lieutenant-Colonel August von Klencke ordered the battalion to deploy for an attack, which was undertaken with such steadiness that the enemy were dislodged from their positions behind the hedges and in the fields on the slope beneath the road to Namur. The Hanoverians advanced at the double towards the hamlet of Piraumont. The artillery fire was considerably weaker at this point, so two guns from Baron Bachelu's Division were pushed forward on the left of the village. However, the speed with which the Lüneburg Battalion advanced almost resulted in their being captured.

A thousand paces to the rear the Grubenhagen Battalion and one of the two companies of Feldjägers attached to the brigade were ordered to march down the gentle slope into the fields of trampled corn, and then through the gap between the pond and the thickset hedges. The men serving with the three remaining battalions sheltered from the artillery fire by lying down in the road. Further to the east, the Brunswick 2nd Light Battalion and the 1st Battalion of the 95th Regiment of Foot, who had been ensconced within the buildings and the adjacent fields at Thyle, joined the attack upon Piraumont. The French *tirailleurs* were driven back, and the impetus of the advance carried the Allied troops into the farm at the centre of the hamlet and beyond to the northern edge of the Bois de l'Hutte. But here they encountered tenacious resistance from the two battalions of the 61e Régiment de Ligne, and were forced to desist.

The French had sustained substantial losses during the various encounters, while the reversal at Piraumont on the right also weakened their hold on the centre. Maréchal Ney deduced that the Allies had been reinforced, and knew that his weary troops would also need to be enhanced if he were to fulfil the emperor's orders. He therefore sent word to Comte d'Erlon to advance with I Corps.

The 69th (South Lincolnshire) Regiment of Foot were deployed in a position north of La Bergerie. Painting by Keith Rocco (Tradition Studios, Virginia)

The fighting at Piraumont, 5:00pm, 16 June 1815

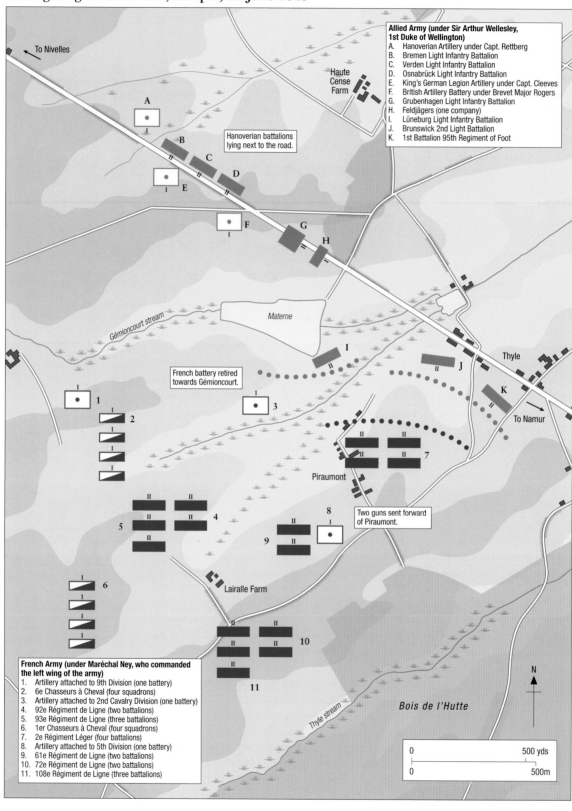

Allied Army (under Sir Arthur Wellesley, 1st Duke of Wellington)
A. Hanoverian Artillery under Capt. Rettberg
B. Bremen Light Infantry Battalion
C. Verden Light Infantry Battalion
D. Osnabrück Light Infantry Battalion
E. King's German Legion Artillery under Capt. Cleeves
F. British Artillery Battery under Brevet Major Rogers
G. Grubenhagen Light Infantry Battalion
H. Feldjägers (one company)
I. Lüneburg Light Infantry Battalion
J. Brunswick 2nd Light Battalion
K. 1st Battalion 95th Regiment of Foot

To Nivelles

Haute Cense Farm

Hanoverian battalions lying next to the road.

Gémioncourt stream

Materne

French battery retired towards Gémioncourt.

Thyle

To Namur

Piraumont

Two guns sent forward of Piraumont.

Lairalle Farm

French Army (under Maréchal Ney, who commanded the left wing of the army)
1. Artillery attached to 9th Division (one battery)
2. 6e Chasseurs à Cheval (four squadrons)
3. Artillery attached to 2nd Cavalry Division (one battery)
4. 92e Régiment de Ligne (two battalions)
5. 93e Régiment de Ligne (three battalions)
6. 1er Chasseurs à Cheval (four squadrons)
7. 2e Régiment Léger (four battalions)
8. Artillery attached to 5th Division (one battery)
9. 61e Régiment de Ligne (two battalions)
10. 72e Régiment de Ligne (two battalions)
11. 108e Régiment de Ligne (three battalions)

Thyle stream

Bois de l'Hutte

N

0   500 yds
0   500m

UNION WITH THE EMPEROR AT SOMBREFFE

A bitter struggle raged in the villages around Ligny, and, to Napoleon's great surprise, the Prussian force was considerably stronger than the single army corps he had expected to encounter. Consequently, at 3:15pm he dictated an order to Maréchal Soult, directing Ney to manoeuvre without delay to the heights of Brye and St Amand and to envelope the right wing of the Prussian Army, in accordance with the order he had issued an hour before. The new order was delivered shortly after 5:00pm, at the moment Maréchal Ney called for Comte d'Erlon to advance with I Corps.

Comte d'Erlon had spent the night at Jumet, to the north of Charleroi, and at first light endeavoured to collect the various divisions belonging to his corps on the north bank of the Sambre River. The 4th Division, commanded by Joseph-François, Comte Durutte, which formed the vanguard of the army corps, had bivouacked between Gosselies and Jumet. The 2nd Division, under the command of Baron François-Xavier Donzelot, was in front of Jumet, along with the 2nd Brigade from the 1st Cavalry Division. However, the 1st and 3rd divisions, led by Barons Quiot du Passage and Pierre-Louis Marcognet, were still at Thuin and Marchienne-au-Pont, close to the border with France, while the 1st Brigade of cavalry from Baron Charles-Claude Jacquinot's Division was further to the rear at Solre-sur-Sambre.

Towards midday Comte d'Erlon received the emperor's instructions, which confirmed that Durutte, Donzelot and Marcognet were to advance with their divisions to Frasnes, while Quiot du Passage was to place his division at Marbais. These movements were to be covered by the cavalry. The orders were immediately communicated to the divisional commanders, who executed them accordingly. Comte Durutte reached Gosselies with the 4th Division at 1:00pm, and because it was impossible to advance any further on the high road, due to the fact that the 6th Division under Jérôme Bonaparte was moving from its bivouac through the town, he awaited the arrival of the remaining divisions within I Corps.

Shortly before 3:00pm the 4th Division resumed its march. Comte d'Erlon and his chief of staff, Baron Victor-Joseph Delcambre, who had sent cavalry patrols forward on the high road, rode ahead of the division with the intention of meeting Maréchal Ney at Frasnes and personally announcing the arrival of I Corps. Unbeknown to Ney, in addition to the order Napoleon had dictated to Maréchal Soult at 3:15pm, which was delivered to the commander of the left wing shortly after 5:00pm, he had also dictated a separate order, timed at 3:45pm, for Comte d'Erlon. In this order Napoleon instructed d'Erlon to bring his four infantry divisions, his cavalry and artillery to the heights of St Amand at once, and by doing so he would save France and cover himself with glory. The order was carried by his aide-de-camp Charles, Comte de la Bédoyère, who found Comte d'Erlon and his suite at the junction of the roads close to Villers Perwin towards 5:00pm. When Comte d'Erlon was informed of the ordered movement, he immediately sent Baron Delcambre forward to inform Maréchal Ney that, in accordance with the emperor's order, the entire corps was moving upon Sombreffe.

It was approaching 5:30pm when Baron Delcambre found Maréchal Ney mounted on his charger upon the heights at La Balcan. Ney was astonished when he learned that I Corps had been ordered to St Amand, but he realized that d'Erlon might have some part to play in the events at this point, and so he instructed Baron Delcambre to return to the corps and explain the critical situation facing the French at Quatre Bras, so that d'Erlon himself could judge how best to serve the nation.

A DETERMINED CHARGE BY THE FRENCH *CUIRASSIERS*

Thereafter, Ney turned to the heavy cavalry commanded by Comte Valmy and, calling for a supreme effort, he ordered the *cuirassiers* to overthrow the Allied infantry and to capture the crossroads. Comte Valmy was hesitant, but realizing the desperate situation he placed himself at the head of the 1er Escardron of the 8e Cuirassiers, alongside Baron Marie-Adrien Guiton, and without allowing the horsemen the time to object to the reckless command he led the five squadrons of the 2nd Brigade into the valley. Due to the position of Gémioncourt, the *cuirassiers* advanced in columns of squadrons to the immediate left of the high road, the three squadrons of the 8e Cuirassiers were on the right, while the two squadrons of the 11e Cuirassiers were on the left.

During the advance Comte Valmy observed an infantry regiment in a hollow, forward of the farm complex, which for some reason was changing from its square formation into line. This was the 69th Regiment of Foot, which had been ordered into this position to support the battalions belonging to Sir Denis Pack's Brigade. Comte Valmy immediately commanded the three squadrons of the 8e Cuirassiers to cross the high road, towards the vulnerable British troops.

The two squadrons of the 11e Cuirassiers continued to advance on the left of the high road, where they soon encountered the 30th Regiment of Foot from Sir Colin Halkett's Brigade, which was safely in square. The horsemen charged vigorously, but they were driven off by well-directed volley fire, although the momentum of the charge threatened the 73rd Regiment of Foot.

François-Étienne Kellerman, Comte Valmy, was a daring cavalry officer noted for his exploits. He commanded III Reserve Cavalry Corps during the campaign, and personally led the 8e and 11e Cuirassiers in a determined charge against the Allied position. Painting by unknown artist. (Musée d'Art et d'Archéologie, Senlis)

The battalion had almost completed its square formation, but had a very limited view of the field due to the tall corn, and when the presence of the French cavalry was made known by the officers, some of the men panicked and sought shelter in the Bois de Bossu. Fortunately for the British infantry the *cuirassiers* did not press home the attack, but on the opposite side of the road the outcome was different.

As the *cuirassiers* approached, the officers of the 69th Regiment of Foot managed to form the battalion into an open column. The Grenadier, No. 1 and No. 2 companies were in the process of closing the square when Brevet Major Henry Lindsay made a grave mistake. He ordered the three companies to halt, wheel about, and to fire at the French horsemen. The salvo staggered the 1er Escadron, but it was insufficient to stop the cavalry from penetrating into the incomplete square, where the fighting intensified. The British were either cut down or fled in disorder to one of the adjacent squares.

A dramatic struggle now took place around the Colours. A party of cavalrymen, which included Maréchal-des-logis Louis-Bernard Massiet, Brigadier Antoine Borgne and two *cuirassiers*, fought their way towards the gallant band in whose care the Colours had been placed. During the contest Ensign George Ainslie, who carried the Regimental Colour, was severely wounded. But he somehow managed to protect the cherished emblem. Ensign Henry Duncan, who bore the King's Colour, was less fortunate. He was covered with wounds and trampled to the ground beneath the hooves of the horse belonging to Cuirassier Pierre Henry, who ripped the Colour from his grasp and carried it victoriously to the rear with several of his comrades.

The French *cuirassiers* had rightfully gained a reputation as ferocious men mounted on very large horses. Print by Martinet (Bibliothèque Nationale de France, Paris)

Elated by their success, the 8e Cuirassiers re-formed and then swept on towards the two squares harbouring the remaining officers and men of the 42nd and 44th, and the 1st and 28th regiments. But as they rode past the hedge of bayonets the French cavalry were greeted by a withering fire from the first square. Comte Valmy hastily ordered the three squadrons to traverse the line and to direct their attack upon the crossroads. That part of the Verden Landwehr Battalion which had been detached to skirmish with the French *tirailleurs* could not retreat sufficiently quickly, and the greater part was either ridden down or taken prisoners. However, the principal recipients of the charge were the Lüneburg Landwehr Battalion, who occupied the position formally held by the highland troops of the 92nd Regiment. The Hanoverians waited until the cavalry were within 30 paces, and then unleashed a devastating volley. Men and horses were sent crashing to the ground, and the whole were thrown into irretrievable confusion. Comte Valmy had his horse shot from beneath him, and like many of his followers, was compelled to retire to the French line on foot.

Having menaced the British and Brunswick formations between the Bois de Bossu and the high road, the two squadrons of the 11e Cuirassiers also charged against the Allied units at the crossroads. But they too were subjected to overwhelming fire, in the form of close-range canister from the four guns of William Lloyd's battery posted immediately in front of the farm at Quatre Bras, as well as a barrage from the battery of horse artillery commanded by Brevet Major Heinrich Kuhlmann, which had arrived in advance of the 1st Division. Indeed, the cavalry sustained such tremendous losses they abandoned the attack and retired to Frasnes.

COOKE ARRIVES WITH THE BRITISH FOOT GUARDS

The Guards reached Nivelles in the early afternoon, and every window was open to witness their advance. It was now that they received an order from Major Egbertus van Gorkum, an officer serving on the General Staff of the 1st Corps, to hasten to Quatre Bras. After quitting Nivelles they marched along the road, and shortly after 5:00pm they reached Houtain-le-Val. The sound of cannon fire was unmistakable, and so the men were ordered to

George Cooke commanded the 1st Division of the Allied Army, which was composed of four battalions of British Foot Guards. Painting by Jan Willem Pieneman (Apsley House, The Wellington Museum, London, UK / Bridgeman Images)

A Grenadier from the 3rd Regiment of Foot Guards painted during the occupation of Paris. Bearskins were only worn by the Grenadier Company, and were not worn on campaign. Print by Genty. (Bibliothèque Nationale de France, Paris)

untie ten rounds of ammunition and to fix their bayonets, while the officers dismounted and fell in to the ranks, with the exception of the field officers. The senior subaltern and the junior ensign, as was the custom, took the King's and Regimental Colours respectively from the colour-sergeants; and with the two light companies of the 1st Brigade under the command of Lieutenant-Colonel Alexander Fraser, Lord Saltoun, in the vanguard of the division, they continued with all due speed towards the field of action. The road was heaving with baggage carts, and they began to encounter wounded officers and men, each of whom informed them that their presence was required. As they approached Quatre Bras the Hereditary Prince of Orange-Nassau galloped along the road and ordered the 1st Brigade to wheel to the right and enter the Bois de Bossu immediately.

Shortly after 5:00pm Prince Bernhard von Sachsen-Weimar had ordered the last of the Nassau troops to retire, as the *tirailleurs* belonging to the 1er Régiment Léger had pushed the Nassau and the skirmishers from the Brunswick Avantgarde back beyond the small rivulet which ran across the Bois de Bossu. The Nassau formed some 300 to 400 paces from the wood, and observed the two light companies under Lord Saltoun entering the coppice at the point it abutted the Nivelles road, and move obliquely towards the enemy.

As the remainder of the 1st Brigade arrived at the crossroads they were immediately employed in supporting the Allied troops. Major-General Peregrine Maitland directed the 1st Guards along the road to the west of the wood, and the 2nd Battalion were ordered to enter, two companies at a time, until the whole of the battalion was committed to the contest. However, the thick undergrowth upset all order and confusion prevailed as the Grenadier and No 1 companies encountered the head of the 2e Bataillon of the 1er Régiment Léger. During the ensuing exchange the leading companies suffered from the fire of their comrades in the 1st Foot Guards, who arrived in succession and engaged the enemy. The 3rd Battalion now moved into the wood on the right of the 2nd Battalion and the French subsequently retired.

Meanwhile, the two light companies led by Lord Saltoun cleared the French from their path with very little resistance and debouched from the wood adjacent to the farm of Gémioncourt, having a deep gulley on their right and a low hedge on their left, behind which the 33rd Regiment was posted. They joined the 2nd and 3rd Battalions, which emerged from the southern extremity of the Bois de Bossu, accompanied by stragglers from various regiments who had been engaged in the fight for possession of the wood before the Guards had arrived, and the whole attempted to form in line. However, the accurate fire from the enemy artillery, which was positioned on the heights close to the farm of Delsot, forced them to withdraw into the wood as far as the small rivulet, and a great many Guards were killed or wounded as the heads of the trees came crashing down upon them. The two commanding officers, colonels Henry Askew of the 2nd Battalion and the Hon William Stuart of the 3rd Battalion, were severely wounded, and the command devolved upon lieutenant-colonels Richard Cooke and Edward Stables respectively.

The fighting in the Bois du Bossu, 6:00pm, 16 June 1815

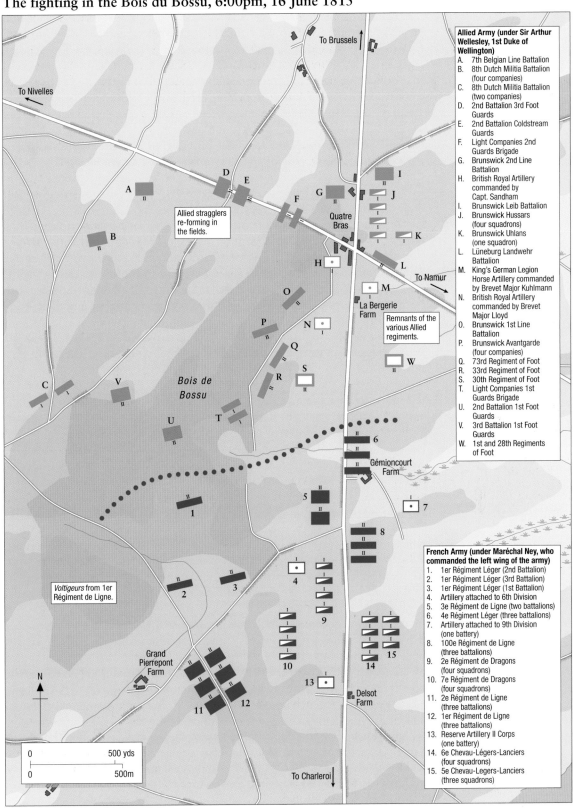

To Brussels

To Nivelles

Allied stragglers re-forming in the fields.

Quatre Bras

To Namur

La Bergerie Farm

Remnants of the various Allied regiments.

Bois de Bossu

Gémioncourt Farm

Voltigeurs from 1er Régiment de Ligne.

Grand Pierrepont Farm

Delsot Farm

N

0	500 yds
0	500m

To Charleroi

Allied Army (under Sir Arthur Wellesley, 1st Duke of Wellington)
A. 7th Belgian Line Battalion
B. 8th Dutch Militia Battalion (four companies)
C. 8th Dutch Militia Battalion (two companies)
D. 2nd Battalion 3rd Foot Guards
E. 2nd Battalion Coldstream Guards
F. Light Companies 2nd Guards Brigade
G. Brunswick 2nd Line Battalion
H. British Royal Artillery commanded by Capt. Sandham
I. Brunswick Leib Battalion
J. Brunswick Hussars (four squadrons)
K. Brunswick Uhlans (one squadron)
L. Lüneburg Landwehr Battalion
M. King's German Legion Horse Artillery commanded by Brevet Major Kuhlmann
N. British Royal Artillery commanded by Brevet Major Lloyd
O. Brunswick 1st Line Battalion
P. Brunswick Avantgarde (four companies)
Q. 73rd Regiment of Foot
R. 33rd Regiment of Foot
S. 30th Regiment of Foot
T. Light Companies 1st Guards Brigade
U. 2nd Battalion 1st Foot Guards
V. 3rd Battalion 1st Foot Guards
W. 1st and 28th Regiments of Foot

French Army (under Maréchal Ney, who commanded the left wing of the army)
1. 1er Régiment Léger (2nd Battalion)
2. 1er Régiment Léger (3rd Battalion)
3. 1er Régiment Léger (1st Battalion)
4. Artillery attached to 6th Division
5. 3e Régiment de Ligne (two battalions)
6. 4e Régiment Léger (three battalions)
7. Artillery attached to 9th Division (one battery)
8. 100e Régiment de Ligne (three battalions)
9. 2e Régiment de Dragons (four squadrons)
10. 7e Régiment de Dragons (four squadrons)
11. 2e Régiment de Ligne (three battalions)
12. 1er Régiment de Ligne (three battalions)
13. Reserve Artillery II Corps (one battery)
14. 6e Chevau-Légers-Lanciers (four squadrons)
15. 5e Chevau-Légers-Lanciers (three squadrons)

The 2nd Brigade reached Quatre Bras, and the battery of foot artillery commanded by Captain Charles Sandham moved forward and took a position immediately to the right of the farm. While the various companies of 3rd Foot Guards were ordered to lie on the ground next to the road, the four leading companies of the Coldstream Guards under Lieutenant-Colonel Daniel Mackinnon marched to the crossroads. Simultaneously, the two light companies commanded by Lieutenant-Colonel James Macdonell advanced along the road and past the artillery pieces which were firing at the enemy. They were led around the northern edge of the wood and into the fields of trampled corn beyond, whereupon a section from the 33rd Regiment of Foot, which had been separated from the main body of the regiment during the earlier French cavalry charges, exited the Bois de Bossu and formed on the road to Nivelles.

Despite the very heavy cannonade, the two light companies continued their advance towards the centre of the Allied position and the farm of La Bergerie. They loaded their muskets and advanced hastily up the rising ground into the farmyard and through the enclosure and the adjoining garden. The shots from the numerous *tirailleurs* rebounded freely off the walls, as Macdonell directed the men through a gap in the hedge closest to the enemy. Brevet Major Heinrich Kuhlmann supported the light companies with the horse artillery attached to the 1st Division, by moving around the outside of the farm and taking a position to the right of the troops. The light guns provided excellent covering fire as the Guards moved over the dead *cuirassiers* and horses, which were lying in heaps about the farm and on the road.

THE CONTEST FOR THE CENTRE INTENSIFIES

Wellington began to feel that the strength of his force was superior to that of his antagonist, and accordingly he ordered the 2nd and 3rd Brunswick Line Battalions to advance from their position between the Bois de Bossu and the high road. They joined in the pursuit of the French infantry with unbridled enthusiasm. However, upon their being threatened by the enemy cavalry both battalions formed square, and the 2nd Line Battalion, with Colonel Elias Olfermann amongst their number, completed the manoeuvre in a manner which evoked the admiration of their leader and all those who witnessed it. The cavalry were repelled, but the three battalions of the 4e Régiment Léger from Baron Jean-Baptiste Jamin's Brigade opened a telling fire on the packed ranks, and the Brunswick troops suffered heavy losses within a very short period of time.

Allied reinforcements moved up in support. Sir Colin Halkett personally led the 30th and 73rd Regiments forward to a position close to the rivulet which ran across the field of battle, while the artillery battery commanded by Brevet Major William Lloyd was united and advanced 600 paces to a new position between the Bois de Bossu and the high road to Charleroi. Nonetheless, the French artillery continued to fire with relentless precision, and Comte Piré moved forward with all of the cavalry at his disposal.

Sir Thomas Picton and the officers and men of his division had endured a torrid time on the battlefield, yet their ordeal was set to continue. As Picton and his suite rode forward to survey the movements of the French cavalry, his horse was hit by a roundshot and collapsed very heavily. The courageous Welshman, who had been severely wounded earlier in the action, was momentarily trapped beneath the dead animal. He was pulled to safety by his aide-de-camp, Captain Charles Gore, and immediately removed to the refuge of the nearby square formed by the 1st and 28th Regiments of Foot.

Comte Piré trotted forward with the 1er and 6e Chasseurs à Cheval, which were greatly diminished in number due to their previous exertions. They moved towards the farm of Gémioncourt and the open ground to the north, which was occupied by the troops of the 5th Division. On this occasion the British soldiers were prepared for the imminent arrival of the French cavalry, although the men within the combined square formed by the 42nd and 44th Regiments had expended almost all of their ammunition. Consequently, an order had been issued for the skirmishers to return to the formation so as to enhance the firepower. But those belonging to the 44th Regiment of Foot, under the command of Lieutenant Alexander Riddick, were unable to do so, as they were cut off by the speed with which the *chasseurs* advanced, and were forced to conceal themselves by lying in the long grass 30 paces from the square.

As the cavalry rode past the front face of the formation they sustained further losses from the intermittent musket fire, but they continued towards the adjacent square of the 1st and 28th Regiments of Foot regardless. Sir Charles Belson, who commanded the 28th, rode back and forth on his bloodied horse inside the square, exhorting his men to remain steady in the face of the charge. He was no doubt satisfied by their conduct, for they delivered a telling salvo into the French horsemen which compelled them to retire upon their reserves, which were stationed just to the north of Gémioncourt. During the episode Sir Thomas Picton had bellowed: 'Twenty-Eight! Remember Egypt!' a reference to the British regiment's glorious past, and an acknowledgement of the fact that the tide of battle had turned.

A British infantryman, supposedly of the 28th Regiment of Foot, illustrated during the occupation of Paris. Print by Genty (Bibliothèque Nationale de France, Paris)

WELLINGTON SEIZES THE INITIATIVE AND ATTACKS

Throughout the course of the afternoon the combatants could clearly hear the roar of the artillery at Sombreffe. The Duke of Wellington subsequently expressed his desire to Generalmajor Karl, Freiherr von Müffling, the Prussian liaison officer attached to his headquarters, to receive a report on the state of the contest, and towards 7:00pm Seconde-Lieutenant Johann von Wussow, an officer serving on the Prussian General Staff, arrived at the crossroads. As Freiherr von Müffling knew that the young officer spoke fluent French, he ordered him to repeat the message that he had been given directly to the duke. The message was concise, and confirmed that when he left the field of battle at 6:00pm the Prussians had occupied most of the villages behind the Ligne stream, which ran across the position, including those of Ligny, St Amand la Haie and Wagnelée. This was despite the determined French attacks which had resulted in the villages being lost and retaken. However, the Prussian losses had been very severe during the

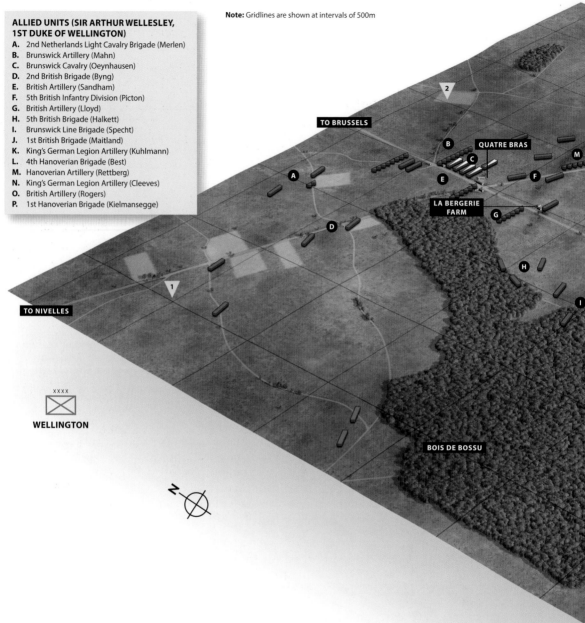

Note: Gridlines are shown at intervals of 500m

ALLIED UNITS (SIR ARTHUR WELLESLEY, 1ST DUKE OF WELLINGTON)

- **A.** 2nd Netherlands Light Cavalry Brigade (Merlen)
- **B.** Brunswick Artillery (Mahn)
- **C.** Brunswick Cavalry (Oeynhausen)
- **D.** 2nd British Brigade (Byng)
- **E.** British Artillery (Sandham)
- **F.** 5th British Infantry Division (Picton)
- **G.** British Artillery (Lloyd)
- **H.** 5th British Brigade (Halkett)
- **I.** Brunswick Line Brigade (Specht)
- **J.** 1st British Brigade (Maitland)
- **K.** King's German Legion Artillery (Kuhlmann)
- **L.** 4th Hanoverian Brigade (Best)
- **M.** Hanoverian Artillery (Rettberg)
- **N.** King's German Legion Artillery (Cleeves)
- **O.** British Artillery (Rogers)
- **P.** 1st Hanoverian Brigade (Kielmansegge)

TO BRUSSELS

QUATRE BRAS

LA BERGERIE FARM

TO NIVELLES

BOIS DE BOSSU

WELLINGTON

EVENTS

1. By 7:00pm the majority of Netherlands troops had withdrawn from the field of battle, with only the 7th Belgian Line and 8th Dutch Militia Battalions remaining to the west of the Bois de Bossu. Most of the Dutch, Belgian and Nassau troops had retired on the road to Nivelles in the direction of Houtain-le-Val, although several battalions headed north of the crossroads in an attempt to replenish their ammunition from the wagons in the adjacent fields.

2. The Allied force was enhanced by the arrival of the Brunswick artillery and the 1st and 3rd light battalions. Their arrival allowed the Duke of Wellington to order the Brunswick Line Brigade to advance between the Bois du Bossu and the high road to Charleroi. It also allowed the troops belonging to the brigade commanded by Colonel Best to advance from their positions behind the road to Namur. They moved into the fields occupied by the beleaguered soldiers of the 5th Division commanded by Sir Thomas Picton, who subsequently retired.

3. At this time the two light companies along with the 2nd and 3rd Battalions of the 1st Foot Guards debouched from the Bois de Bossu, to the north of Grand Pierrepont. But here they were assailed by the fire from the French *tirailleurs* belonging to the 1er Régiment Léger, who had taken positions behind the ditches and hedges, and they were subjected to fire from the French artillery stationed at Delsot. The combined assault forced the Guards to retire into the wood to a position close to the small rivulet which traversed the field.

4. The attack upon the hamlet of Piraumont by the Hanoverian troops of Count Kielmansegge's Brigade and the Brunswick 2nd Light Infantry had forced the four battalions of the 2e Régiment Léger to retire from the buildings and the adjacent fields, into the Bois de l'Hutte. This withdrawal was covered by the 61e Régiment de Ligne and the divisional artillery, and prevented the Allied force from entering the wood. However, the French withdrawal weakened their hold on the centre, particularly as this part of the battlefield had proven difficult for their cavalry to manoeuvre.

THE FRENCH ADVANCE

The situation at Quatre Bras, 7:00pm, 16 June 1815

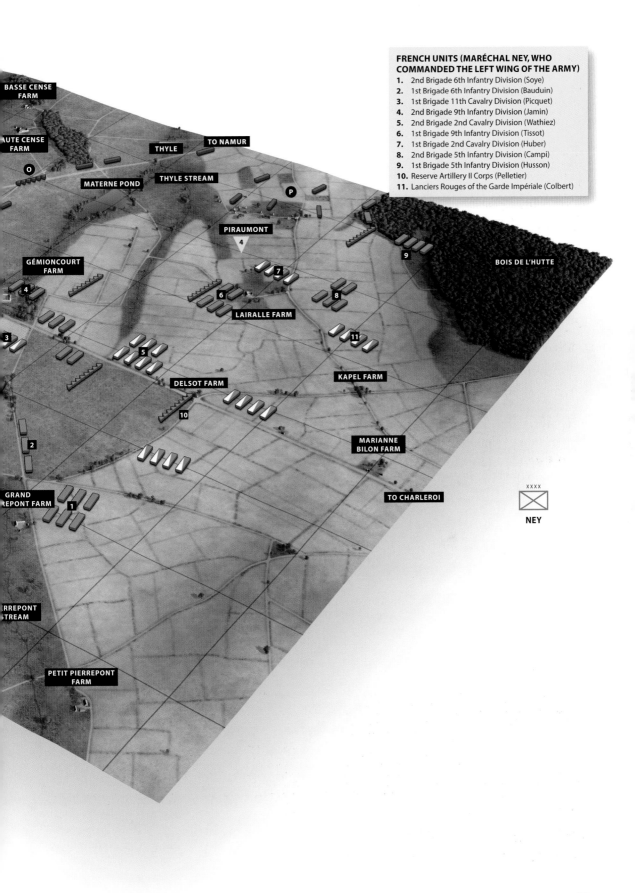

FRENCH UNITS (MARÉCHAL NEY, WHO COMMANDED THE LEFT WING OF THE ARMY)

1. 2nd Brigade 6th Infantry Division (Soye)
2. 1st Brigade 6th Infantry Division (Bauduin)
3. 1st Brigade 11th Cavalry Division (Picquet)
4. 2nd Brigade 9th Infantry Division (Jamin)
5. 2nd Brigade 2nd Cavalry Division (Wathiez)
6. 1st Brigade 9th Infantry Division (Tissot)
7. 1st Brigade 2nd Cavalry Division (Huber)
8. 2nd Brigade 5th Infantry Division (Campi)
9. 1st Brigade 5th Infantry Division (Husson)
10. Reserve Artillery II Corps (Pelletier)
11. Lanciers Rouges of the Garde Impériale (Colbert)

BASSE CENSE FARM

HAUTE CENSE FARM

THYLE

TO NAMUR

MATERNE POND

THYLE STREAM

PIRAUMONT

BOIS DE L'HUTTE

GÉMIONCOURT FARM

LAIRALLE FARM

DELSOT FARM

KAPEL FARM

MARIANNE BILON FARM

TO CHARLEROI

GRAND PIERREPONT FARM

xxxx
NEY

PIERREPONT STREAM

PETIT PIERREPONT FARM

fighting, and as the prospect of support from IV Korps had disappeared completely, the best the Prussians could hope to achieve was maintenance of their current positions until the onset of night.

Having explained this to the duke, von Wussow requested, on behalf of the Prussian high command, that the British undertake a strong offensive, which they believed would prevent Napoleon from making any further attacks upon their positions. The Duke of Wellington listened intently and then replied in French. He asked the staff officer to inform Graf Neidhardt von Gneisenau, in whose name the message had been delivered, that it had been very difficult for him to resist the onslaught by the superior French forces up until this point, but as he had been suitably reinforced he believed that with the troops at his disposal he would take the offensive and endeavour to support the Prussians at Sombreffe as requested. The Prussian staff officer departed and the duke immediately issued orders to the troops at Quatre Bras.

Shortly thereafter, the Brunswick 1st and 3rd light battalions and the Brunswick artillery arrived at the crossroads. These were the first of the Allied troops to be put in motion. The two infantry battalions moved forward to support the Brunswick troops between the Bois de Bossu and the high road, while the artillery took a position slightly to the rear of the road to Namur, on the left of the farmhouse at Quatre Bras.

On the left of the Allied line at Piraumont, the Hanoverian troops from Count Friedrich von Kielmansegge's Brigade attacked the two battalions of the 61e Régiment de Ligne defending the edge of the Bois de l'Hutte. Having been reinforced by the Bremen Light Infantry Battalion, the Lüneburg, Grubenhagen and one company of Feldjägers steadily drove the French into the wood, and then deployed in a manner that would enable them to hold the position without venturing further.

Along the line the Allies seized the initiative and the French infantry were compelled to retire. The light companies of the 2nd Guards Brigade pursued the enemy across the field, but their advance was opposed by the French cavalry. Lieutenant-Colonel James Macdonell of the Coldstream Guards, who commanded the two companies, found it necessary to counter the threat by forming the men into a compact square. From his elevated position on horseback in the centre of the square he directed the Guards as the cavalry moved aside and the French artillery fired at their formation. Shells fell within several paces of the outward ranks and exploded with a tremendous blast, but the full destructive force of the fire was foiled by the timely movements prescribed by the skilful commander. The battery of horse artillery

As the Duke of Wellington began to feel the strength of his force superior to that of his enemy he seized the initiative. The massed ranks of French troops were slowly pushed back. Print by Paolo Boscetti. (Rijksmuseum, Amsterdam)

from the King's German Legion commanded by Captain Heinrich Kuhlmann joined the fray, having moved forward from La Bergerie. Three guns were unlimbered between the high road and the Bois de Bossu, adjacent to the compact square, while the remaining three guns were positioned further to the east, on the opposite side of the road, in order to deliver oblique fire upon the French infantry formation to the rear of Gémioncourt. Within minutes the cannon were responding to the enemy artillery fire by spewing shot and shells.

In the Bois de Bossu the two battalions of 1st Foot Guards had re-formed close to the small rivulet, and with the Brunswick Avantgarde on their left, they advanced in line through the wood until they reached the hollow track which ran along the eastern edge. While the experienced Brunswick marksmen remained behind the cover of the trees, the Guards moved into the cornfields between the wood and the high road. The officers ran forward a short distance to a loose hedge, and the men emerged from the wood and extended in line on the same ground. However, the three battalions of the 1er Régiment Léger, which were lying in wait in the adjacent fields, immediately opened a continuous fire on the British. Ensign James, Lord Hay, aide-de-camp to Major-General Peregrine Maitland, was killed and Lieutenant-Colonel William Miller of the 3rd Battalion was mortally wounded. The officers carrying the Colours were particularly targeted, and the ground was soon covered with the dead and wounded. A state of some considerable confusion prevailed.

Comte Piré observed the encounter and ordered his remaining *lanciers* to charge from their concealed position in the low ground to the east of Grand Pierrepont. They were joined by the *dragons* from the reserve cavalry corps commanded by Comte Valmy and the Lanciers Rouges of the Garde Impériale. The horsemen burst upon the Guards and inflicted severe casualties. Instinctively, the British troops sought protection in the hollow track along the edge of the wood, and with supporting fire from the Brunswick Avantgarde, they succeeded in driving the French cavalry back.

The brief engagement momentarily threatened to stop the Allied advance, but the sheer weight of numbers that the Duke of Wellington could call upon, aligned with the length of time the French infantry had been in the field, had begun to tell.

THE FIGHTING AT QUATRE BRAS ENDS IN STALEMATE

Shortly after 8:00pm the first of the British cavalry reached the crossroads. These were the officers and men of the 23rd Light Dragoons, which formed part of the brigade commanded by Major-General Wilhelm von Dörnberg stationed at Mons. The cavalry had ridden that day from the frontier where they had been on outpost duty, and immediately upon their arrival a detachment was sent forward to reconnoitre the enemy and their movements to the south of the Bois de Bossu. Further Allied reinforcements arrived in the form of the 1st and 2nd Battalions of the 1st Nassau-Usingen Regiment, under the command of Baron August von Kruse. The infantry took a position on the right of the high road, close to the buildings at Quatre Bras, where they awaited the arrival of their comrades in the 3rd Battalion.

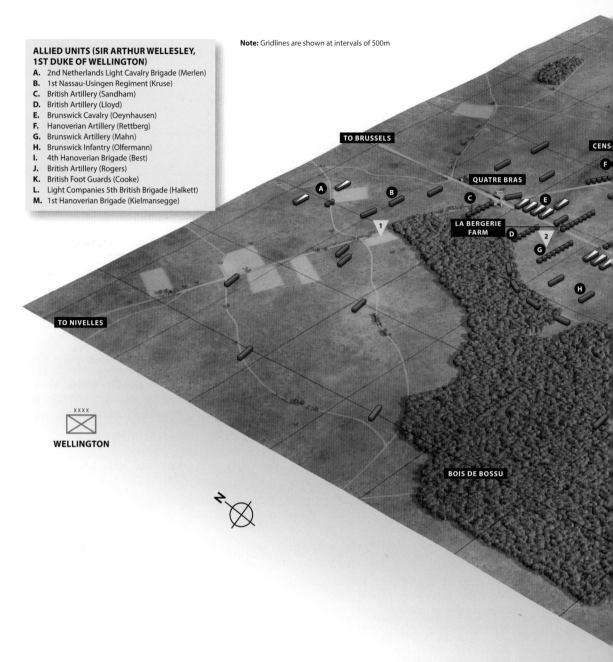

Note: Gridlines are shown at intervals of 500m

ALLIED UNITS (SIR ARTHUR WELLESLEY, 1ST DUKE OF WELLINGTON)

A. 2nd Netherlands Light Cavalry Brigade (Merlen)
B. 1st Nassau-Usingen Regiment (Kruse)
C. British Artillery (Sandham)
D. British Artillery (Lloyd)
E. Brunswick Cavalry (Oeynhausen)
F. Hanoverian Artillery (Rettberg)
G. Brunswick Artillery (Mahn)
H. Brunswick Infantry (Olfermann)
I. 4th Hanoverian Brigade (Best)
J. British Artillery (Rogers)
K. British Foot Guards (Cooke)
L. Light Companies 5th British Brigade (Halkett)
M. 1st Hanoverian Brigade (Kielmansegge)

TO BRUSSELS

CENS

QUATRE BRAS

LA BERGERIE FARM

TO NIVELLES

XXXX
WELLINGTON

BOIS DE BOSSU

▼ EVENTS

1. By 11:00pm the fighting had ceased and the majority of the Allied troops were ordered to lie upon the field of battle among the dead and the wounded. Allied reinforcements continued to arrive, including the three battalions of the 1st Nassau-Usingen Regiment under Major-General August von Kruse. They took a position to the north of the crossroads. Their compatriots in Dutch service had already left the field, with the exception of stragglers from the battalions which had been engaged earlier in the battle.

2. Most of the Brunswick infantry took positions between the high road and the Bois de Bossu. In this way they formed the right wing of the Allied line, with the support of the British Foot Guards, who were stationed further to the south. The Brunswick cavalry was advanced to a position adjacent to the sheep farm of La Bergerie, while the artillery belonging to the Brunswick Corps moved to the south of the buildings.

3. The centre of the Allied line comprised the 28th and 32nd Regiments of Foot from Sir Thomas Picton's 5th Division, the remnants from Sir Colin Halkett's 5th British Brigade, the militiamen from Carl Best's 4th Hanoverian Brigade, and the two King's German Legion artillery batteries. These were enhanced by the 23rd Regiment of Light Dragoons. To the east the hamlet of Piraumont was maintained by Count Friedrich von Kielmansegge's 1st Hanoverian Brigade and the officers and men of the Brunswick 2nd Light Battalion.

4. As the exhausted troops of Comte Reille's II Corps retired towards Frasnes they were replaced by those of I Corps. The two brigades of the 1st Infantry Division formed on the right of the line, with the 1st Brigade in the Bois de l'Hutte. The divisional artillery was pushed forward to provide cover. The two brigades of the 2nd Division took positions in the centre and on the left of the line. The artillery moved onto the heights at Delsot, where there was a wide field of vision. The extreme left of the French line was held by the Lanciers Rouges of the Garde Impériale, before they retired to the haven of Frasnes.

THE CLOSING STAGES

The situation at Quatre Bras, 11:00pm, 16 June 1815

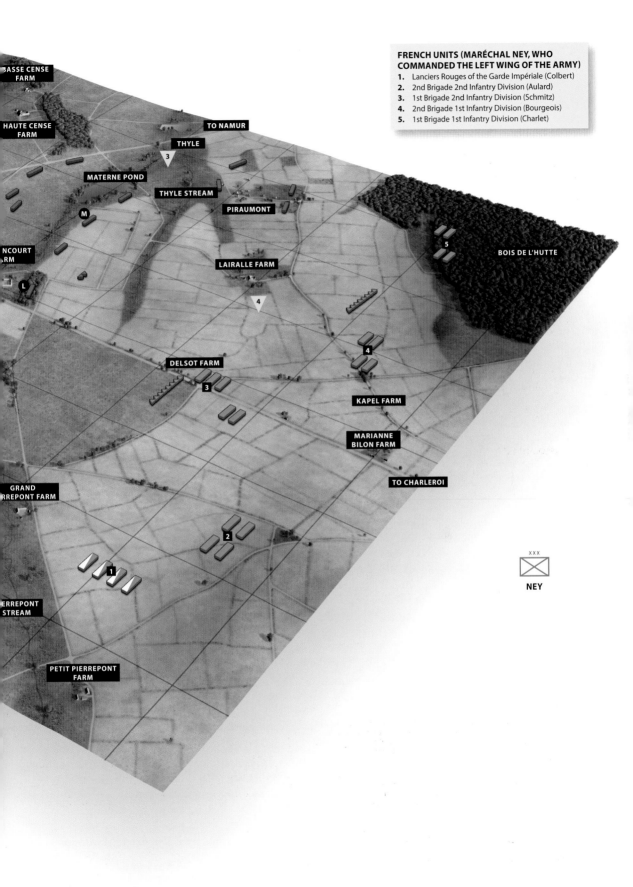

FRENCH UNITS (MARÉCHAL NEY, WHO COMMANDED THE LEFT WING OF THE ARMY)

1. Lanciers Rouges of the Garde Impériale (Colbert)
2. 2nd Brigade 2nd Infantry Division (Aulard)
3. 1st Brigade 2nd Infantry Division (Schmitz)
4. 2nd Brigade 1st Infantry Division (Bourgeois)
5. 1st Brigade 1st Infantry Division (Charlet)

BASSE CENSE FARM

HAUTE CENSE FARM

TO NAMUR

THYLE

MATERNE POND

THYLE STREAM

PIRAUMONT

M

NCOURT RM

LAIRALLE FARM

BOIS DE L'HUTTE

5

L

4

DELSOT FARM

3

KAPEL FARM

MARIANNE BILON FARM

GRAND RREPONT FARM

TO CHARLEROI

2

NEY

1

ERREPONT STREAM

PETIT PIERREPONT FARM

85

The farm of Gémioncourt had been the point from where the French had launched their attacks on the Allied centre, but now it became the focus of the Duke of Wellington's attention. With the support of the Lüneburg Landwehr from Colonel Carl Best's Brigade, the composite Light Infantry Battalion from the 5th British Brigade, commanded by Sir Colin Halkett, moved forward. This movement was supported by the 30th Regiment of Foot and two of the guns from the horse artillery under Captain Kuhlmann. The three battalions of the 1er Régiment Léger, to the west of the Gémioncourt, between the high road and the Bois de Bossu, retired slowly towards the farm complex to gain support on their right flank from the 4e Régiment Léger, and this movement enable the remainder of Sir Colin Halkett's troops, along with the 1st and 2nd Brunswick line battalions, to advance steadily. As the British Guards and Brunswick Avantgarde lined the hollow track along the south-west edge of the wood, the Allies could advance in line without fear of being assailed by enfilading fire, although the threat the French cavalry offered to the infantry had been admirably demonstrated during the course of the day, and the Allies remained extremely diligent. However, the French were disinclined to continue the contest. They slowly withdrew from the farm buildings and the immediate vicinity, and were hastily replaced by the British light infantrymen.

To all intents and purposes the battle of Quatre Bras was over, and the Allied troops had maintained their ground, albeit with a degree of good fortune and without being able to render any direct assistance to the Prussian Army. Towards 9:00pm the Duke of Wellington and his sizeable entourage retired to Genappe, where his headquarters were established at the Hôtel du Roi d'Espane. Here, he dictated several orders concerning the deployment of outposts and the communication between the two wings of the Allied Army during the night. The Hereditary Prince of Orange-Nassau left the battlefield at the same time as the duke, and rode with Baron Constant-Rebècque to the headquarters of the 2nd Netherlands Division in Nivelles, before retiring to his quarters within the residence of Madame de Robin.

Having ensured that the Duke of Wellington's orders had been complied with in full, the various divisional and brigade commanders retired, but on the battlefield the troops laid down on their arms amidst the dead and the dying. At Piraumont the Hanoverians of the Verden Light Infantry Battalion replaced the Grubenhagen and Lüneburg battalions, which had been hard-pressed in the earlier contest. An outpost was established to the north of the Bois de l'Hutte by two companies from the Osnabrück Battalion, while the remaining troops of Count Friedrich von Kielmansegge's Brigade were held in reserve. The Brunswick 2nd Light Battalion took a position further north, in the fields between the hamlet and the village of Thyle.

In the centre, to the west of the high road, the troops of Sir Thomas Picton's 5th Division were relieved by the various Landwehr battalions belonging to Colonel Carl Best's Brigade. The 28th, 32nd and 79th regiments took positions to the south of the Namur road, while the remaining officers and men of the 1st, 42nd and 44th regiments withdrew completely in rear of the crossroads. The Brunswickers deployed immediately to the south of Quatre Bras, close to the Bois de Bossu, ready to advance towards Gémioncourt, if necessary.

On the right of the Allied line, Major-General Peregrine Maitland led the 3rd Battalion 1st Foot Guards to the southern edge of the Bois de Bossu, and having thrown out picquets he directed the 2nd Battalion to withdraw to the Nivelles road, in consequence of the severe losses the battalion had sustained during the fighting. The Coldstream Guards subsequently moved down through the wood and formed on the left of their comrades in the 1st Guards. The Brunswick Avantgarde, who had played such an important role in supporting the British Guards during the fighting, retired to a position closer to the other Brunswick battalions south of the crossroads.

As the veil of darkness slowly enveloped the battlefield Maréchal Ney ordered the entire force at his disposal to withdraw to the heights of Frasnes, and to establish a strong line of outposts at this point. Thereafter, he retired to his headquarters at the Maison Dumont in Gosselies, where at 10:00pm he wrote a short account of the events to Maréchal Soult. Ney praised the valour of the troops under the command of Comte Reille and the *cuirassiers* led by Comte Valmy, but he declared that he had been deprived of a fine victory by the order which summoned Comte d'Erlon and I Corps to St Amand.

In the meantime, reports arrived from Comtes Reille and Valmy concerning the role of their troops during the battle. Having read these the weary *maréchal* dined with Comte de Flahaut, the emperor's aide-de-camp, who had remained with him at Quatre Bras throughout the day. They awaited their instructions from the imperial headquarters at Fleurus, and details of the outcome of the fighting with the Prussians.

NAPOLEON IS TRIUMPHANT AT SOMBREFFE

The emperor had surveyed the battlefield from his position at the windmill of Naveau to the north of Fleurus as Comte Vandamme, at the head of III Corps, aided by the 7th Division under Baron Jean-Baptiste Girard, which was detached from II Corps, attacked the hamlet of St Amand to the west. In the centre, Comte Gérard and IV Corps were engaged with the Prussians in the village of Ligny, while to the east, the French cavalry commanded by Maréchal Grouchy threatened the defenders of Boignée and the village of Sombreffe on the road to Namur. In accordance with the emperor's favourite tactic, the Garde Impériale had been held in reserve on the heights at Fleurus, and they were supported by the heavy cavalry corps commanded by Édouard, Comte Milhaud.

Following a desperate struggle the French carried the villages of St Amand and St Amand la Haie, but amidst the ferocious fighting Baron Girard was mortally wounded. Prussian reinforcements were immediately sent forward, and as the contest escalated more were required to replace the heavy losses they incurred. The French were gradually driven out of the buildings of St Amand and the Prussians regained possession of most of the village. However, the attack was renewed with support from the *tirailleurs* of the Jeune Garde. Along the line Comte Gérard and IV Corps attempted to gain a foothold in the village of Ligny, but the Prussian troops were entrenched, and they defended the position with such determination that successive attacks were repelled. Undaunted by the failure the French rallied, and augmented by the horse artillery of the Garde Impériale, they bombarded the village and assaulted the Prussian positions from two sides. More of the Prussian reserves were committed to the contest, but despite their heroic efforts the situation became critical.

Napoleon prepared the Garde Impériale, so as to deliver the decisive blow upon the weakest point in the Prussian line. However, towards 6:30pm the emperor received a message from Comte Vandamme, stating that a dense column had appeared a league to his left and was turning the French flank. The intelligence caused an immediate suspension of the attack in this quarter, and a reconnaissance party was sent to discover the strength and disposition of the unidentified body.

Comte d'Erlon had followed the order he received from the emperor at 5:00pm to forsake his role at Quatre Bras and to march with his entire corps to St Amand. Having taken the precaution of sending his Chief of Staff, Baron Victor-Joseph Delcambre, to inform Maréchal Ney of his movements, he had marched towards the battlefield at Sombreffe. As before, the 4th Infantry Division commanded by Joseph-François, Comte Durutte, formed the vanguard of the army corps, along with the troops of the 2nd Brigade belonging to the 1st Cavalry Division under Baron Charles-Claude Jacquinot. These were followed by the 2nd and 3rd Infantry divisions of Barons François-Xavier Donzelot and Pierre-Louis Marcognet, while the 1st Division under Quiot du Passage brought up the rear.

The leading elements of Comte Durutte's Division and the majority of the cavalry had reached the outskirts of the battlefield, opposite Wagnelée, shortly after 6:00pm, and it was their arrival, in rear of III Corps, which caused consternation on the left of the French line. Napoleon was surprised by the intelligence, as he had expected any reinforcement to arrive from the direction of the Namur road. Subsequently, Comte d'Erlon's unexpected arrival afforded the Prussians the chance to re-form and delayed the final attack that the emperor had been preparing.

Instantly recognizable by their lavish uniforms, the *chasseurs à cheval* principally undertook the scouting and escort duties that were vital within the French Army, Print by Martinet. (Bibliothèque Nationale de France, Paris)

Yet the difficult decisions facing Comte d'Erlon and I Corps were far from over, for it was now that Baron Delcambre returned to the corps with information from Quatre Bras. He explained the situation and recounted the message he had been given by Maréchal Ney, which allowed the commander of I Corps to decide upon the correct course of action. Comte d'Erlon sought the views of his staff officers, and based upon these he sent orders to Durutte and Jacquinot to remain in their positions and to display the utmost caution, while he would march with the remainder of the corps back to Quatre Bras. However, it would be 9:00pm before the vanguard reached Frasnes. This critical decision was undoubtedly one of many which determined the outcome of the campaign.

After a delay of more than half an hour the French renewed the attack on St Amand and continued the relentless struggle in Ligny, where by 8:00pm they had captured most of the village. The Prussian centre was exposed, and as a thunderstorm shrouded the battlefield in darkness, Napoleon launched the Garde Impériale. Six infantry battalions moved forward to join with those already engaged, followed by the duty

Movements of Comte d'Erlon's Corps, 4:00–9:00pm, 16 June 1815

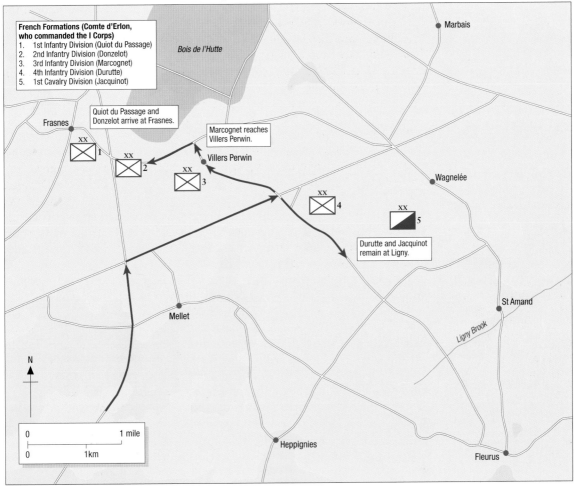

French Formations (Comte d'Erlon, who commanded the I Corps)
1. 1st Infantry Division (Quiot du Passage)
2. 2nd Infantry Division (Donzelot)
3. 3rd Infantry Division (Marcognet)
4. 4th Infantry Division (Durutte)
5. 1st Cavalry Division (Jacquinot)

Quiot du Passage and Donzelot arrive at Frasnes.

Marcognet reaches Villers Perwin.

Durutte and Jacquinot remain at Ligny.

squadrons and the *cuirassiers* of the 14th Cavalry Division under Lieutenant-général Delort. With support from the artillery the Prussian centre was pierced and the position carried, despite a desperate charge from three regiments of cavalry led by Feldmarschall Blücher. During the fighting the Prussian leader had his horse shot from beneath him and was pinned to the ground by the dead animal. Fortunately, one of his staff witnessed the fall and remained with him until he could be carried to safety.

Of greater significance to the Prussian leader was the onset of night, which prevented the French from profiting from their victory, as only a few of their horsemen reached the road to Namur. But the confusion within the Prussian Army was manifest, and although the two wings remained intact, along with their command structure, the withdrawal to a position of safety was undertaken in considerable disarray. The majority of the troops retreated as far north as Wavre before they were rallied and some semblance of order restored.

The French were in possession of the battlefield, although they had not gained the decisive victory the emperor had sought. Furthermore, Napoleon was unaware of the outcome of events at Quatre Bras.

AFTERMATH

When Comte d'Erlon returned to the field of battle at Quatre Bras he was summoned to an interview with Maréchal Ney at his headquarters in Gosselies, so as to explain the circumstances surrounding the movements he had undertaken with I Corps. Before he departed, Comte d'Erlon ordered the 1st and 2nd Divisions to relieve the exhausted troops of II Corps, who subsequently withdrew to Frasnes and lit their campfires.

News of the engagement at Quatre Bras and the plight of the Allied troops reached Brussels, as the first of the walking wounded arrived in the capital. The residents were shocked to learn of the engagement and the ensuing losses. A considerable number of the severely wounded men were taken to Nivelles, while others received treatment in the field hospitals which had been established in the nearby villages. However, the battlefield was strewn with the bodies of hundreds of dead and dying men and horses, and the eerie silence of the night was broken only by the calls of the wounded in their many languages for water.

During the course of the night the Allied Army was reinforced by the steady arrival of the British cavalry. The 2nd King's German Legion Brigade, commanded by Baron Christian von Ompteda, also reached the field of battle during the hours of darkness, but the roads to Brussels and Nivelles remained choked with wagons, and resounded to the constant rattle of the artillery being moved into position.

Towards 4:00am the leading battalions of the 54e and 55e Régiments de Ligne forced a passage to the edge of the Bois de l'Hutte, and engaged the detachment from the Osnabrück and the troops of the Brunswick 2nd Light Infantry Battalion

posted behind thickset hedges to the north of the wood. The attack was followed by several others. On each occasion the Allies allowed the French to advance to within 500 paces of their positions before engaging in counterfire and pursuing the enemy a short distance. The Bremen Light Infantry Battalion was advanced to support their comrades, but they began to run perilously short of ammunition, until more was sent forward in small barrels. With the grey light of dawn the fighting slowly subsided.

From his headquarters at the Hôtel de le Roi d'Espagne, the Duke of Wellington issued supplementary orders to the Allied Army. The 2nd Division and the Reserve Artillery were directed to Quatre Bras, while the 4th Division was ordered to move upon Nivelles. Thereafter he retired for the night, ready and willing to unite with the Prussians and to renew the contest the following morning. Unbeknown to the duke the Prussians had sent a courier with details of their withdrawal the previous evening, but the unfortunate officer had been shot by a French patrol while attempting to deliver the message. Consequently, Wellington and his subordinates were unaware of the precarious situation which confronted them.

A contemporary print showing the walking wounded arriving in Brussels. On the day of battle many of the Allied troops wounded at Quatre Bras made their way to Nivelles. Colour aquatint by Robert Bowyer (www.historicalimagebank.com)

THE BATTLEFIELD TODAY

The passage of time has naturally ensured that the battlefield at Quatre Bras has changed since the fateful events of 16 June 1815. But visitors to the site may still enjoy many of the principal landmarks which featured during the course of the fighting, and recapture the atmosphere of the day.

Unlike the battlefield at Mont St Jean, scene of the battle of Waterloo, Quatre Bras was not the subject of intense tourism. It remains a very small village, although the populace has increased considerably in number and there are many more buildings and significant levels of traffic. This is a major benefit for a visitor to the area, as the main road forms part of the bus route running between Brussels and Charleroi.

The crossroads themselves bear witness to many of the changes. Monuments have been erected to the combatants and those who fell. Sadly, the large farmhouse and barn has been allowed to fall into a state of ruin, and is destined to be demolished. A plaque honouring the Netherlands troops which had been placed on the outside wall has subsequently been removed for preservation and display at another venue in the future.

This aerial view of Quatre Bras is from immediately south of the crossroads. The road on the left of the picture leads to Nivelles, while that on the right leads to Ligny and Sombreffe. (Photograph by Jean-François. Schmitz)

Farther along the road to Nivelles is a monument to the Belgian soldiers who died at Quatre Bras, which was inaugurated in 1926. This was supplemented by a modern monument to the Dutch and Belgian cavalry, who fought alongside one another during the campaign, which was erected in 1990. Serving members of the respective armies, who trace their lineage to the various cavalry regiments, gather each year to commemorate their deeds. A monument to the British and Hanoverian troops, which was erected at the instigation of the 8th Duke of Wellington in 2002, is opposite.

Perhaps the most notable change immediately south of the crossroads is the area of farmland where the western half of the Bois de Bossu once stood. Unfortunately, the trees within this part of

The farm of Petit Pierpont, formally known as Petit Pierrepont, along with the farm of Grand Pierrepont, held by the Nassau troops from Bernhard von Sachsen-Weimar's Brigade at the start of the action. (Photograph by Jean-François Schmitz)

the wood were so badly damaged during the battle that they were felled in the aftermath of the campaign. Part of the wood still remains, adjoining a golf course which has a club house at Golf du Pierpont, formally known as the farm of Grand Pierrepont. The farm of Petit Pierpont is also extant.

To the south of the crossroads, west of the road leading from Brussels to Charleroi, is a monument to the Duke of Brunswick, the most senior officer within the Allied Army to fall at Quatre Bras. Mounted by a lion holding a shield, it has a lengthy inscription to the duke. The monument was erected in 1890 and is in desperate need of repair.

A little further south is Gémioncourt, the most engaging spot on the battlefield, which remains a working farm. It was the scene of intense fighting and the point from which the French launched many of their attacks on the centre. It is therefore fitting that in 1988 a plaque was placed at the gates in memory of the French soldiers who lost their lives on 16 June 1815.

The farm of Gémioncourt was the scene of heavy fighting at the beginning of the contest, and was the position from where the French launched most of their attacks upon the crossroads. (Photograph by Jean-François Schmitz)

FURTHER READING

Anton, J., *Retrospect of a Military Life during the Most Eventful Periods of the Last War* Edinburgh, 1841

Arcq, A., *La Bataille des Quatre-Bras, 16 Juin 1815* Annecy-le-Vieux, 2005

Bas, F. de and T'Serclaes de Wommersom, J. de, *La campagne de 1815 aux Pays-Bas, d'après les rapports official Néerlandais* Brussels, 1908

Beamish, N. L., *Geschichte der Königlich Deutschen Legion* Hanover, 1837

Boulger, D. C., *The Belgians at Waterloo* London, 1901

Bowden, S., *Armies at Waterloo* Arlington, 1983

Chesney, C., *Waterloo Lectures* London, 1868

Clerk, A., *Memoir of Colonel John Cameron, Fassifern, Late Lieutenant-Colonel of the Gordon Highlanders, or 92nd Regiment of Foot* Glasgow, 1858

Dellevoet, A., *The Dutch-Belgian Cavalry at Waterloo* The Hague, 2008

Drouet d'Erlon, J. B., *Le maréchal Drouet Comte d'Erlon. Notice sur la vie militaire écrite par lui-même et dédiée à ses amis* Paris, 1844

d'Elchingen, Duc, *Documents inédits sur la campagne de 1815* Paris, 1840

Franklin, J. (ed.), *Waterloo: Hanoverian Correspondence – Letters and Reports from Manuscript Sources* Ulverston, 2010

——, *Waterloo: Netherlands Correspondence – Letters and Reports from Manuscript Sources* Ulverston, 2010

Gardner, D., *Quatre Bras, Ligny and Waterloo* London, 1882

Glover, G. (ed.), *Letters from the Battle of Waterloo: The Unpublished Correspondence by Allied Officers from the Siborne Papers* London, 2004

Harvard, R., *Wellington's Welsh General: Life of Sir Thomas Picton* London, 1996

Henckens, E. (ed.), *Mémoires se rapportant à son service militaire au 6e regiment de chasseurs à cheval francais de févriér 1803 à août 1816* La Haye, 1910

Hofschröer, P., *The Waterloo Campaign: Wellington, His German Allies and the Battles of Ligny and Quatre Bras* London, 1998

Jameson, R., *Historical Record of the Seventy-Ninth Regiment of Foot, or Cameron Highlanders* Edinburgh, 1863

Kelly, C., *A Full and Circumstantial Account of the Memorable Battle of Waterloo* London, 1817

Knoop, W. J., *Quatre Bras en Waterloo.* Schiedam, 1865

Külbel, E. C., *Die letzten Augenblicke unsers Durchlauchtigsten Herzog Friedrich Wilhelm bei Quatrebras den 16 Juni 1815* Celle, 1865

Löben Sels, E. van, *Bijdragen tot de krijgsgeschiednis van Napoleon* The Hague, 1842

Martinet, A., *Jérôme Napoléon, roi de westphalie* Paris, 1902

Miller, D., *The Duchess of Richmond's Ball* Staplehurst, 2004

Muilwijk, E., *Quatre Bras, Perponcher's Gamble: 16th June 1815* Bleiswijk, 2012

Pawly, R., *Les Lanciers Rouges de la Garde: historique du 2e Régiment de Chevau-Légers Lanciers de la Garde Impériale* Brussels, 2008

Pflugk-Harttung, J. von, *Die Vorgeschichte der Schlacht bei Quatre Bras* Berlin, 1902

Répécaud, C. M., *Napoléon à Ligny et le maréchal Ney à Quatre Bras. Notice historique et critique* Arras, 1849

Robinson, M., *The Battle of Quatre Bras* Stroud, 2009

Ross-Lewin, H., *With the Thirty-Second in the Peninsula and Other Campaigns* Dublin, 1904

Siborne, H. T. (ed.), *Waterloo Letters. A Selection from Original and Hitherto Unpublished Letters Bearing on the Operations of the 16th, 17th and 18th June, by Officers Who Served in the Campaign* London, 1891

Siborne, W., *History of the War in France and Belgium in 1815; Containing Minute Details of the Battles of Quatre Bras, Ligny, Wavre and Waterloo* London, 1844

Sichart, A. and R. von, *Geschichte der Königlich Hannoverschen Armee* Hanover and Leipsig, 1898

Thiriar, J., *Waterloo* Brussels, 1914

Trefcon, T. J., *Carnet de campagne de Colonel Trefcon, 1793–1815* Paris, 1914

Uffindell, A., *The Eagle's Last Triumph. Napoleon's victory at Ligny* London, 1994

Wachholtz, L. von, *Geschichte des herzoglich Braunschweigischer Armeekorps in dem Feldzuge der alliierten Mächte gegen Napoleon Buonaparte in Jahre 1815* Braunschweig, 1816

Wacker, P., *Das herzoglich-nassauische Militär, 1813–1866* Taunusstein, 1998

Wüppermann, W. E. A., *Quatre Bras en Waterloo* Amsterdam, 1913

INDEX

Figures in **bold** refer to illustrations.